The Peaceful Nursery

The Peaceful Nursery

Preparing a Home for Your Baby

with Feng Shui

Laura Forbes Carlin & Alison Forbes

Photographs by Tamara Muth-King

Delta Trade Paperbacks

THE PEACEFUL NURSERY
A Delta Trade Paperback / March 2006

Published by Bantam Dell
A Division of Random House, Inc.
New York, New York

Book design by Virginia Norey

Library of Congress Cataloging in Publication Data
Carlin, Laura Forbes.
The peaceful nursery : preparing a home for your baby with feng shui /
Laura Forbes Carlin and Alison Forbes.
p. cm.
ISBN-13: 978-0-385-33894-3
ISBN-10: 0-385-33894-5
Includes index.
1. Nurseries. 2. Feng shui in interior decoration. 3. Interior
decoration—Psychological aspects. I. Title.
NK2117.N87 C37 2006
747.7'.7 22   2005051938

Printed and bound by Toppan, China, 2005
Published simultaneously in Canada

www.bantamdell.com

TOP   10   9   8   7   6   5   4   3   2   1

This book is dedicated to sweet baby James who is pure love and inspires peace, wonder, and joy in each and every moment.

And to our beautiful, brilliant, and loving mother Jane for her boundless energy and infinite capacity to give.

Acknowledgments

We have been blessed with extraordinary people in our lives, many of whom have helped us along this journey. Our heartfelt thanks and gratitude ...

To David Kuhn for his time, energy, thoughtful guidance and for making this possible!

To Billy Kingsland at Kuhn Projects for his expert assistance.

To the Bantam Dell Publishing group, particularly Danielle Perez for welcoming us to Bantam Dell, and Shannon Jamieson Vazquez for her enthusiasm, commitment, and thoughtful insights.

To Tamara Muth-King who understood this project so well and helped bring it to life with her beautiful photographs.

To Karine Gallet and Gabriele Wilson, great friends and talented designers, for their creative contributions.

To Mary Cordaro for her expert advice.

To Terah Kathryn Collins, the founder of the Western School of Feng Shui, for being such a gifted and generous teacher.

To the other great teachers who have inspired, guided, and encouraged us: David Allen, Reverend Michael Beckwith of Agape, Alex Demaras, Drs. Ron and Mary Hulnick of the University of Santa Monica, Becky Iott, Gurmukh Kaur Khalsa, Davi Kaur Khalsa, and Denise Linn.

To all our family who gives meaning to our lives. Especially to our father Walter Forbes, to Robert Saltonstall, and to Richard and Phyllis Carlin.

And more than ever to Scott Carlin, a great brother-in-law and an amazing husband for keeping us grounded with his patience, strength, and unconditional love.

To all of our friends, too numerous to mention here, for their love and encouragement. Special thanks to our friends who have contributed throughout the process: Laura Aryeh, Robin Berman, Laura Berk, Kristin Edwards, Kari Falls, David and Dane Findley, Haley Fischer, Ashley Locke, Pamela Neville, Dawn Parouse, Marnie Pomerantz, Jessica Redmond, Ingrid Roper, Stephanie Scott, Pamela Sparkman, Andrea Stanford, Cara Tapper, and Camy Toth, and to Mark Bailey for his vote of confidence.

To the helpful people in our lives who offer us great support: Dr. Soram Khalsa, Sant Kaur Khalsa, Dr. Jim Blechman, Kathleen Calabrese, Dr. Jay Gordon, Judy Falaise, Dr. Kathryn Gill, Letty Diaz, and particularly to Kit Wilkins, for continuously bringing us back to our center.

To the following people for sharing their wonderful homes and nurseries: the Salzman Family, the Berman Family, the Stanford Family, the Grosfeld Family, the von Krusenstjerna Family, Vanessa Parise, and Andrea and Marc.

And finally to Spirit, the source of all.

Contents

Introduction:

Welcoming Your Baby Home *1*

Chapter One: At Home *5*
You and Your Home 7
Designing Your Life 8
Feng Shui 9
Healthy Home 10
Intention 11
Trust Your Intuition 17
Quick Tips 18

Chapter Two: Preparing Your Home *19*
Clearing Your Clutter 20
Living with What You Love 21
Types of Clutter 23
Clearing as Meditation 26
Twelve Steps to Clutter Clearing 26
Organization 31
Storage 31

Changing Habits That Create Clutter 33
Teaching Your Children to Clear Clutter 34
Quick Tips 36

Chapter Three: Preparing the Room *37*
Choosing a Room 37
Renovations and Repairs 40
Color 41
Paint 43
Floors and Lighting 44
Cleaning 46
Energy Cleansing 47
Blessing 50
Quick Tips 51

Chapter Four: Comfort and Safety *53*
Safety 53
Healthy Nursery 55
Healthy Furniture 57
Comfortable Furniture 58
Furniture Placement 59
Your Comfort Zone 61
Energy Flow 64
Quick Tips 67

Chapter Five: What You Will Need *69*
Preparation and Organization 70
The Nursing Area 71
The Changing Area 73

The Bathing Area 75
The Sleeping Area 77
The Play Area 79
Clothes 82
Other Things to Consider 83
Travel 86
Quick Tips 88

Chapter Six: Enhancing the Nursery *89*
Decorating from the Heart 89
Enhancements 91
Nursery Enhancements 92
Energy Enhancements 96
Imitating Nature 99
Balance 100
Big Rooms and Small Rooms 101
Patterns and Themes 102
Harmonious Home 103
Quick Tips 104

Chapter Seven: Designing Your Life *105*
The Bagua 105
Bagua Areas 106
Applying the Bagua 109
"Missing" Areas 112
The Bagua and Your Life 113
Nursery Bagua 114
Nursery Bagua Enhancements 115
Quick Tips 119

Chapter Eight: A Good Night's Sleep *121*
Sleep 121
Routine 122
Sleeping Rooms and Playrooms 124
Light 128
Sound 129
Energy Cleansing 129
Receiving Help 130
Adult Bedrooms 132
Quick Tips 135

Chapter Nine: Preparing Yourself *137*
Deciding You're Ready 137
Gratitude 138
Self-Nurturing 140
Being the Most of Who You Are 141
Building a Relationship with Your Baby 143
Being in the Moment 144
The Forty Days 146
Asking for Help 147
Your Partner and Expectations 148
Everything Changes 150
Role of Parent and Maker of Homes 151
Quick Tips 152

Bibliography 155

Resources 159

Index 165

The Peaceful Nursery

Welcoming Your Baby Home

Your home can be your sanctuary—a place of renewal, a source of support, and a cause of inspiration. You learn about and express yourself through your home. Therefore it makes sense that one way to prepare for parenthood is by preparing your home for your new baby. During pregnancy you are, literally, full of life. As your body is expanding, your capacity for love is expanding, and your consciousness is expanding, your home also needs to expand in its own way. As you create a nursery and prepare your home for your baby, you will be making space in your life, both physically and emotionally, for the most special gift—a child. Parenting is never easy, but we believe that the more prepared you are and the more your home and life are designed to support you, the less overwhelming it will be.

As sisters, we have not only shared a home, but also a passion for everything about the home. We have always believed that a home can be so much more than simply a shelter; it can also support and shape your life. When we first learned about Feng Shui, the ancient Chinese art of placement, we realized that although it was unfamiliar to us, we had in many ways been practicing it our entire lives, so becoming Feng Shui consultants felt like a natural progression.

Fundamentally, Feng Shui is about arranging your surroundings to enhance your life. Our consulting focuses on the intuitive, universal aspects of Feng Shui that can be applied in our contemporary Western culture. Feng Shui is full of practical ideas to help you design a home that nurtures your mind, body, and spirit.

With the knowledge we acquired studying Feng Shui and life coaching techniques we began helping our clients to not only design their homes, but also to recognize their needs, clarify their goals, and then create an environment that supports them in successfully meeting those needs and attaining those goals. We began to see just how connected our homes are to our physical, mental, emotional, and spiritual well-being. Our homes cannot be separated from the

quality of our lives. If we wish to experience good health, our homes should be healthy. If we desire more peace, our surroundings should be peaceful. Designing our homes can be so much more than just creating a beautiful space—we are in fact designing our lives.

We were so enthusiastic about helping people recognize the power of their surroundings that we co-founded *The Art of Everyday Living,* a home and lifestyle consulting company, specializing in what we call "Life Design," a unique service that combines Feng Shui, life coaching, interior decorating, and healthy living. Over the years, we witnessed the positive effect Life Design has had on our clients' lives, as well as on our own. We also learned just how helpful our homes can be when experiencing a major life change, such as changing careers, moving, or getting married.

So when Laura began to prepare for one of the biggest events in her life, the birth of her son James, we turned to her home. By creating a room for James, we learned how to apply these principles to a nursery. Together we shared our ideas on how to create a comfortable, peaceful, healthy, and beautiful nursery as well as an organized and prepared home that would best support a transition into parenthood. Realizing just how challenging and powerful this transition can be inspired us to share what we'd learned about preparing a nursery for the benefit of other expectant parents.

Whether you have a large room or small nook available to create a nursery doesn't matter: you can create nurturing surroundings for your baby in any space. Don't worry about making it perfect—there is no "right" way to make a nursery. It is all about the spirit and love that you bring to the process.

Your home, and specifically the nursery, will be your baby's next womb. Your baby will learn about the world by interacting with this special space. The first few weeks and months of a newborn's life lay the foundation for your relationship together. It is important to make sure that this time is as healing and loving as possible. If you wish the experience to be filled with peace, love, health, and joy, your environment should reflect these same qualities. Our hope is that this book will help ensure that your and your baby's physical, emotional, and spiritual needs are met by helping you create the most supportive environment possible.

As a parent you know that your child is watching you and learning from you in every moment, and the best gift you can give your child is to be the best version of yourself that you can. Creating a healthy, functional, comfortable, and beautiful home can help you achieve that goal by boosting your energy and offering support, inspiration, and peace. And as you change your home to accommodate your new baby, you will change yourself. Re-creating your home and designing your nursery will give you the opportunity to re-create and design your new life as a parent. This holistic and mindful process of preparing the nursery will help you prepare for the exciting and challenging miracle of welcoming a baby into this world.

Laura and Alison

Chapter One

At Home

Home is as much a feeling as it is a physical place. "It's good to be home," "home sweet home," and "welcome home" are all expressions that strike a deep emotional chord. "Feeling at home" is synonymous with feeling content, comfortable, and secure. It is important to your health and happiness that the physical space you call home provides you with this sense of comfort and security. Creating a home—and more specifically, a special place for your baby—that will give both you and your child this sense of peace is essential.

There is no better time to create a home that supports and nourishes you and your family than when preparing for the birth of a baby. The transition into parenthood can be one of the most extraordinary, yet also demanding, times in your life. As you adjust to your new role as a mother or father, your home can become a great source of support. An organized, healthy home and a peaceful, beautiful, comfortable nursery can help you function with ease and grace. In addition, as you design the nursery and make space for your new baby, you will also take an inner journey that will prepare you for parenthood: as you change your home, you too will change. Your home will become a vehicle for becoming more conscious about who you are, what your priorities are, what kind of parent you want to be, and what kind of children you want to raise.

For a newborn, the significance of the nursery is even more profound: the nursery is your baby's next womb. An enchanted, peaceful, and cozy nursery will give your baby the security and comfort to thrive. Some of your baby's first interactions with you and the world will take place in this room. By creating a

A bassinet placed near your bed is a gentle way to welcome your baby home.

nursery filled with healthy, happy, and loving energy, you're building the foundation for a healthy, happy, and loving relationship with your baby.

You and Your Home

Your home has an enormous influence on your physical, emotional, mental, and spiritual well-being. An organized, beautiful, and toxin-free environment can boost your energy, promote good health, and support your dreams, while a disorganized, cluttered, and uncomfortable space can deplete your energy, undermine your ability to succeed, and dampen your spirits.

Your home tells the story of who you are, what you enjoy doing, how you are feeling, and who you spend your time with. Your surroundings are an outward manifestation of your inner experience. Your home is a reflection of you. For example, if you're feeling a little down, you might find yourself unconsciously creating a gloomy environment by shutting the curtains or allowing your home to become messy. On the other hand, if you come back from a vacation reenergized and with a "new outlook on life," you may choose to reflect your new state of mind by displaying souvenirs or photographs from your vacation. The pictures on your wall, the food in your refrigerator, the objects you have stored in your closet, how you decorate (or don't decorate) are all things that can tell you something about yourself. What story is your home telling about you? Take a moment to "read" your home by observing your surroundings. Do the objects you have chosen to surround yourself with reflect your interests, hobbies, and habits? If the answer is yes, then go one step further and ask yourself if you are happy with that reflection. If the answer is no, ask yourself why not?

Being conscious of your environment is so important because your surroundings have the ability to influence your life. For instance, a clean, clutter-free desk may help you pay your bills on time, which may in turn affect your finances. A comfortable dining area may encourage more family meals, thereby shaping a closer relationship with your family. A restful, quiet nursery will help your baby sleep, allowing you to also get more rest, which will then affect your family's health and happiness. What's in your home and how it's arranged can affect some of the most important aspects of your life.

Designing Your Life

Once you appreciate the power of the connection between your surroundings and your life, you can use this new understanding to organize and decorate your home so that it supports you in building the life you desire. As you design your home, you have the opportunity to design your life. What better time than when preparing to welcome a new baby to create the life you envision for yourself and your new family?

The most effective changes in your home will result not only in the physical transformation of your surroundings, but also in a transformation of your mind, body, and spirit. Your home offers an opportunity for change because it is a tangible reflection of your innermost feelings, yet it is separate enough that you can step back and be objective. It is often easier to address the state of one's home than one's state of being. For example, a disorganized home may be easier to identify and change than a disorganized life.

It is easy to only focus on the big events—such as holidays, celebrations, or entertaining out-of-town guests—yet it is the small everyday moments that make up the majority of your life. What seem like tiny annoyances or disturbances in your home can actually affect your well-being in much greater ways. Clutter on the kitchen counter may prevent you from cooking nutritious meals, which over time could affect your health. Searching frantically for your keys each morning might make you consistently late for work, which could then affect your career. Your home should nurture you by supporting your daily rituals. Your living room should be comfortable and lively so that your friends feel welcome. Your bedroom should promote peaceful sleep so that your immune system has time to recoup and your health is maintained.

Designing your home is both an inner and outer process. By making changes in your outer surroundings, you are supporting a change on the inside. If you want to bring more serenity into your life, you'll want to bring objects, colors, and art into your home that are relaxing. You could bring in a small fountain if you are calmed by the sound of water, or light candles if watching the flicker of a flame brings you a sense of tranquility. Whatever you choose to "bring" to your home, you are also "bringing" to yourself. To further achieve your goal of bringing more peace into your life, think about the changes you'd like to make within yourself, such as reducing stress, maintaining a positive outlook, or seeking clarity about personal issues. Perhaps you will choose to meditate each day, or to start each morning writing down everything that is "on your mind" to help you feel more at peace. As you bring peace and harmony into your home you are simultaneously fostering inner peace and harmony. As your environment becomes more and more a reflection of who you are, your state of mind and physical surroundings seem to blend. The more aligned your inner and outer world, the more you feel "at home."

Feng Shui

Many cultures recognize the link between your home and your life. In India, the five-thousand-year-old design practice called Vastu holds that you must first create harmony in your environments in order to experience harmony within yourself. Many Native American rituals revolve around connecting to the land and giving thanks to Mother Earth. In Germany, Bau-biologie, the study of how your environment and the materials in your home and office affect your health, holds that you must live in healthy buildings in order to experience optimal health. Feng Shui is the three-thousand-year-old Chinese practice of making positive changes in your environment to produce positive changes in your life. All of these practices have evolved similar holistic approaches to design, the core of which acknowledges the connection between one's environment and one's well-being.

Feng Shui revolves around the universal principle that everything is made up of energy, including your body, your thoughts, and the empty space surrounding you. Even objects you may consider inanimate, such as a table or a rock, are made up of moving molecules and send out their own unique vibration. Your own energy is affected by all the energy that surrounds you. The goal is to help positive energy flow through your home in a way that enhances your life. Feng Shui embraces the idea that, just as different pressure points in acupuncture correspond to specific parts of the body, different areas of your home are associated with different areas of your life. These areas include health, family, love, relationships, career, wealth, fame, helpful people, children, creativity, knowledge, and self-cultivation. So when you improve the energy in part of your home, you're also improving part of your life.

Although Feng Shui may seem complex, its philosophy includes common-sense practices and simple suggestions such as keeping your environment clean and organized, clearing clutter, arranging furniture so you can move easily from room to room, surrounding yourself with things you love that reflect and support your goals, and putting safety and comfort first by making sure your home is healthy and functional as well as beautiful. Fundamentally, Feng Shui is about making a home that you thoroughly enjoy—a home that supports your dreams and nurtures your mind, body, and spirit.

Healthy Home

A basic tenet of Feng Shui holds that your physical environment is in essence an extension of your body and therefore how you care for your home is just as important as how you care for yourself. Think of all the care women put into nurturing their bodies while pregnant. You need to give the nursery the same kind of consideration. Just as a woman does not put toxins, such as alcohol and cigarette smoke, into her body during pregnancy, you should not put anything toxic in the nursery. With all the best intentions, many parents buy all new furnishings for the nursery, furnishings that contain chemicals that, especially when new, may release unhealthy fumes into the air of the nursery.

Paying attention to air quality and the chemicals found in your home is particularly important when preparing for a new baby. Babies' immature organs are less able to cope with the toxins in their environment than those of adults. Children enjoy touching everything around them; eventually either their hands or random objects wind up in their mouths, exposing them to even more chemicals.

People are becoming increasingly aware of the numerous chemicals in the environment. Many people know that most produce is treated with pesticides that remain on the food all the way to the kitchen. As a result, many people wash their fruits and vegetables and are becoming more conscious of the importance of buying organic food. People are also more aware than ever that industrial pollutants and pesticides from farm fields can contaminate water supplies, to the point where drinking bottled water and using water filtration systems in homes is commonplace. In today's world you also need to pay as close attention to the materials that you use to build, decorate, and clean your home as you do to the food you eat and the water you drink.

Taking small steps to create a healthy home will make a big difference, so don't worry if you can't make big changes in your home today—do what you can. Even small changes in your environment can significantly impact your life. You may even decide to just start with one room; and what better room than the nursery where your baby will spend more than a third of his or her early life? A number of different approaches and alternative products to help you create a healthy nursery will be discussed throughout this book, and can also be found listed in the resource section.

Intention

To create a home that nourishes your mind and spirit as well as your body, you first need to discover what feeds your spirit by getting in touch with your dreams and identifying your goals. You are constantly attracting people and things in your life through your personal energy, thoughts, and consciousness. There is a universal principle that your thoughts create your reality. What you put out into the world comes back to you, or in other words: like attracts like. When you are feeling good about yourself you are more apt to attract positive people and opportunities. When you have clear intentions and focus you are more likely to realize your goals. Have you ever had the experience of hearing about something for the first time and then within the next month you hear about it ten more times? Once you focus your attention on something it will start to appear in your life, so instead of fixating on what is wrong in your life, concentrate on what *is* working in your life and be optimistic about attaining your dreams and goals. By clarifying your intentions, defining your goals, visualizing positive outcomes, and creating an environment filled with symbols of your goals, you will manifest your dreams with ease.

The first step toward getting in touch with your dreams and clarifying your goals is to create a Life Design. Begin by writing down all the areas in your life you wish to enhance, such as your family, your friends, your home, your health, your finances, and your career. You may also wish to have a special area devoted just to your baby, including pregnancy, the birth experience, and the first few months at home. The next step is to create a written list of successful outcomes for each area, called affirmations. Affirmations are most effective when written in the present tense. Begin with the words "I am" and finish the sentence with your highest aspirations. The process of writing down your intentions is one of the most effective things you can do to create the life you desire. Writing down your goals sends a powerful message to the universe that is usually answered in extraordinary ways.

The following is an example of a Life Design.

Remember that as you are writing down your affirmations you are in fact designing your life. You may alter your Life Design to fit your unique circumstances. Be specific and add as many details and affirmations as you want. This is your vision!

Relationship:

I am enjoying a loving and affectionate relationship with my partner.
I am communicating with my partner with ease and clarity.
I am supported by my partner in being all of who I am and I support my partner in being all of who he is.

Family and Friends:

I am grateful for my supportive and loving family.
I am easily attracting new like-minded friends into my life.
I am energized by the time I spend with my friends.
I am happily finding time to see my friends at least once a week.

Health:

I am experiencing optimal physical, mental, emotional, and spiritual health.
I am easily making time to care for myself.

Home and Lifestyle:

I am easily transforming my home into a healthy, peaceful, beautiful sanctuary.
I am enjoying an organized, streamlined, and comfortable home that meets all of my family's needs.
I am thoroughly enjoying creating a cozy nursery.
I am experiencing grace throughout my days.

Finances:

I am experiencing financial prosperity.

I am gratefully receiving abundance in all its forms.

Career:

I am enjoying a successful career that is in alignment with my values and purpose.

I am inspired and fulfilled by my work.

Pregnancy and Birth Experience:

I am experiencing a healthy, easy, comfortable, and happy pregnancy.

I am experiencing an easy and healthy labor and delivery.

My baby and I are experiencing optimal health.

Each and every moment of my experience from driving to the hospital to
*   bringing my baby home is filled with ease, grace, and helpful people.*

I am with my baby at all times.

I am experiencing a quick and full recovery.

I am quickly and effortlessly returning to my pre-pregnancy weight.

Parenthood:

I am easily and joyfully transitioning into parenthood.

I am so grateful for my healthy and happy baby.

I am communicating with my baby with ease, grace, and clarity.

I am trusting my instincts and following my heart.

I am easily creating a comfortable routine for me and my baby that includes
*   good sleep, happy awake times, and graceful outings.*

I am having fun and celebrating my relationship with my baby.

You can enrich your Life Design in a variety of ways. For example, it is help-ful to make a list of the things you value most such as peace, love, health, abun-dance, simplicity, joy, kindness, beauty, and creativity. You can also support yourself in manifesting your goals within a certain time frame by making a list of your ten-year goals, five-year goals, and one- to two-year goals. To empower yourself from day to day, consider a list that includes ongoing daily, weekly, monthly, and yearly goals such as: meditate each day, exercise three times a week, read a book a month, vacation two times a year, etc. Most likely your Life Design includes a great deal of successful outcomes. Keep in mind that things may go a little differently than planned, but often the outcomes are even greater than you could have imagined.

The next step is to stay focused on realizing your goals. There are several ways to do this, including reviewing your goals, taking action steps, meditating or praying, visualizing, creating visual reminders, and letting go.

Review your intentions. It is helpful to periodically review your Life Design. Try reading it before you start your day or before you fall asleep at night.

Take action steps. Reviewing your Life Design will help you align your actions with your intentions. Action steps are defined as anything you may need to do to support your goals. For example, if you would like to feel comfortable about your birth experience you may wish to take an action step such as participating in a childbirth class.

Meditate or pray. A powerful form of prayer is called "affirmative prayer," which recognizes that everything you desire on some level already exists—you just need to ask that it be experienced, revealed, or manifested. An easy way to do this is to express gratitude for all the good that you know you are calling forth. By being thankful you are acknowledging that what you desire is now manifesting in your life. You may also want to meditate. Meditation helps you quiet your mind and let go of "mental clutter," thereby making you more available in the present moment. While meditating, don't focus specifically on your Life Design, focus instead on the *feeling* your Life Design evokes. If the feeling is happiness, simply meditate on the word happiness; if the feeling is peace, meditate on the word peace.

Visualize. The visualization process focuses your attention on the best possible outcome for any situation. Many athletes and coaches use visualization techniques before a game by imagining they are playing at the best of their ability, and winning. The following describes a simple visualization process:

- *Find a quiet place to sit or lie.*
- *Take a few minutes to relax by focusing your attention on your breath.*
- *Imagine yourself in a future situation and then imagine you and whomever you are with surrounded by a gentle, loving light.*
- *Imagine yourself experiencing success and happiness each step of the way. What happens? What do you touch, taste, smell, hear, or see? How do you feel?*
- *Spend a few minutes enjoying the sensations and emotions of joy and success.*

Create visual reminders. You can bring your dreams into your home by creating a visual reminder of your goals. For example, if you wish to travel somewhere, you might place a picture of the place you wish to travel to in your home. Each time you walk by, you will be reminded of your dreams. Another possibility would be to create an arrangement on a table or a shelf that might include a special box for your Life Design, candles, plants or flowers, and other cherished objects, quotes, books, or photographs.

Let go. A powerful technique is to simply let go. Once you have clear intentions and a heartfelt purpose expressed in your Life Design, simply let go of your plan. Sometimes when you hold on too tightly to one vision, you miss other opportunities. Instead, trust that all will turn out well and surrender to the present moment.

If you find that your dreams are not being realized, it is usually because you're not clear about your goals. Every once in a while, review your Life Design to make sure that it's still in alignment with your dreams.

Trust Your Intuition

Most likely you will find you are already intuitively integrating many of the ideas in this book into your life. Anything that looks good and feels right to you will enhance your home and life. However, if anything suggested in this book doesn't feel right to you, listen to your instincts. There is no "right" way to create a nursery just as there is no "right" way to parent. Parents have wonderful instincts—"mother's intuition" is a widely acknowledged reality—so listen to yourself and trust that in the end whatever you choose to do out of love for your child will most likely be right for both of you.

As you prepare your home for your baby's arrival keep in mind that the most important thing your baby needs is love: to be held, respected, cared for, talked to, and cherished by his parents. The nursery is an expression of this love. How you relate to yourself as you create the nursery is as important as the end result. Experiencing stress, physically wearing yourself out, or putting pressure on yourself while you prepare your home and nursery will not benefit you or your baby. It would be better to do less, and do it in a way that reflects the positive energy you want to create. As you bring love and peace into the process of creating a nursery, you are also bringing love and peace to your family's life. The feeling of being "at home" is a feeling both you and your children can take with you, wherever you go.

Quick Tips

• Imagine that your home is telling the story of your life. What is it saying? Do you like what it is saying? Is the story an accurate reflection of who you are? Consider removing anything from your home that does not reflect who you are or who you want to be.

• Take some time to write your responses to the following questions:

   * How do you feel about your home?

   * What area of your home most appeals to you, and why?

   * What area of your home least appeals to you, and why?

   * What are the qualities of your ideal home?

   * What are the qualities of your ideal nursery?

   * What areas of your life are working well for you?

   * What areas of your life, if any, are presenting challenges?

   * List in order of priority the areas in your life that you would like to enhance.

• Create a Life Design based on the list you just wrote. Begin by writing down each area of your life that you would like to enhance, such as health, relationships, career, family, pregnancy, creating the nursery, the first few months at home with your baby, etc. Compose a series of affirmations for each area and read your Life Design every night before you go to bed.

• Take a moment to connect with your intuition. You already know exactly what needs to be done to create a home that nurtures you and your family.

Chapter Two

Preparing Your Home

Before you focus on the nursery it is important to take a look at your home as a whole. Your life is about to change dramatically, so it makes sense that your home will need to change too. Take this time to make space for your baby. If you already feel busy, and already have a full schedule, imagine what it will be like when you are responsible for your baby's needs, meals, appointments, schedule, and everything else! The more you simplify and organize your own life before your baby arrives, the less overwhelmed you will be by the demands of being a new parent, and the more time you will have to enjoy with your child. Take the time to simplify and get organized now. Once the baby is born you'll be too busy—just finding the time to complete everyday tasks, or do things you used to take for granted such as exercising, socializing, or going out to dinner can be difficult. Often new parents find adjusting to the lack of personal time challenging.

One of the most effective solutions to this problem is to clear clutter and get organized. A disorganized, cluttered home can drain your energy, waste your time, and make your daily routines burdensome and difficult, while a clean, clutter-free, organized home boosts your energy, helps you complete tasks efficiently, and makes your daily routines flow quickly and smoothly. As a new parent you will want to conserve and create as much time and energy as possible. We can all identify with the frustration of being unable to find our keys or losing an important document due to clutter, but imagine how your frustration

The simplicity of a clutter-free nursery inspires a sense of calm and peace.

could increase when compounded by the needs of a baby. If there are areas in your home that you feel need to be put in order, it's best to take care of them now.

Clearing Your Clutter

Clutter is anything in your home that you don't use regularly or that you don't treasure. When you hold on to things that you no longer enjoy, or things that no longer reflect who you are now, you take up precious time and space, thereby preventing new and better things that you *do* want from coming into your life. In other words, clutter keeps us tied to the past and delays the realization of our dreams. When you clear your clutter, you have the opportunity to examine (and let go of) where you have been, take inventory of where you are, and then set intentions for where you want to go. You clear the way for new people, ideas, material blessings, and opportunities to come into your life.

There is no better motivation for clearing clutter than becoming a parent. Try to anticipate the reality of parenting and look at each object in your home and say to yourself, "I am a parent now—do I have time for this?" Chances are if you have not found time to fly-fish, take ballet, bake fresh bread, or go horseback riding before you had a child, you certainly will not find the time once the baby arrives. So out with the rod, toe shoes, bread-maker, and jodhpurs! This clearing will help make time and space for the activities that are really important to you.

Again, the most important reason for you to clear clutter is to maximize personal time and preserve much-needed energy. Clearing clutter actually helps you save time because the fewer objects you have, the less you have to take care of, fix, maintain, and clean. Think how much time and energy it takes to clean, store, repair, dry-clean, buy, order, return, tailor, and learn how to use our possessions. The amount of stuff in people's lives today is overwhelming. There is a great deal of truth to the expression "Our possessions end up owning us." The more clutter you clear, the more time you have to focus on what is truly precious: time with your new baby, and time to rest and relax.

Living with What You Love

A great way to guarantee that your home supports you is to make sure you love everything in it. Broken appliances, things you don't like, or objects associated with negative memories can, whether you're conscious of them on a daily basis or not, block the flow of energy in your life, frustrate you, and dampen your spirits. When you look at the contents of your home from this point of view you can see why it is essential to live with things that are in good condition and bring you joy. Possessions you love, useful items, beautiful objects, and things you associate with positive memories will boost your energy. In turn, you may express your gratitude for material blessings by making sure they are well cared for and have an organized space of their own. Terah Kathryn Collins in her book *The Western Guide to Feng Shui: Room by Room* says, "The more you practice living with what you love, the more exciting and affirmational your life will become."

Take a moment to look around and see what your home is saying about you. The image of yourself you see reflected back at you through your home is so powerful that it not only influences how you feel each day, it actually determines your future as well. In the same way that you might begin to doubt your abilities if a coworker told you over and over that you weren't capable of succeeding, your home could be sending you a similar message. By surrounding yourself with things you don't love, that are not in good condition, or things that you feel are second-rate, you're subconsciously telling yourself you don't deserve better. Rooms you can barely walk through, where you can't find what you're looking for, or that contain broken objects, do not boost your self-esteem. You may have had the experience of being late for an important meeting because you can't find anything to wear, or you can't find your briefcase, or your broken garage door slows you down. Individually these small annoyances may seem trivial, but over time they begin to create stress, cause arguments, and can eventually deplete your self-esteem. On the other hand, you will feel peaceful and empowered when you live in an organized home that helps you flow easily through your daily routines. When beautiful, ordered surroundings are reflected back to you, your self-esteem is strengthened. For these reasons letting go of clutter and organizing your home is an act of self-care and self-love. Insist on surrounding yourself with things that reflect your current goals and your highest idea of who you are. Keep in mind that sometimes you first need to say *no* to what you don't want in your life in order to make space for the things you do want.

Clear your space of things that do not represent your dreams or empower you to fulfill your goals. Actually walk through your home and look at each object in every room and ask yourself the following questions:

- Does this object reflect who I am now in my life?
- Does it support my current goals?
- Do I need it? (Is it useful?)
- Do I love it?

You should be able to answer yes to at least one of the above questions about every item in your home. If your answer is no to all of the above questions, consider selling the object, giving it away, or throwing it out. You may also take this time to do some physical cleaning and make sure that all items in your home are in good repair. This process provides an opportunity to let go of anything that no longer serves you or represents who you are now.

Types of Clutter

Fear-Based Clutter

Whenever you find yourself saying, "I am keeping this (fill in the blank) because I'm afraid I won't have enough money next year to buy one I really like, or because I'm afraid there could be a fire, or because I'm afraid I might get sick again," you have fear-based clutter. These fear-based thoughts are a signal to let it go. Whatever you put your attention on will tend to manifest. Your thoughts, words, and actions create your reality. You will not want to keep objects that encourage you to focus on negative scenarios such as a financial loss, illness, or natural disaster. Instead, let the item go with the positive thought that you trust that you will be provided for and that all your needs will be met. Karen Kingston, in her book *Clear Your Clutter with Feng Shui,* says the number one reason people accumulate clutter is because of "just in case" scenarios. An example would be someone keeping crutches "just in case" he breaks his leg again, or someone keeping suits in her closet for over ten years "just in case" she stopped making it as an artist and needed to get a day job again. "Just in case" scenarios are based on fear. Go around your home and take a few moments to find out what your clutter is saying to you. If you are keeping anything that is attached to a doomsday scenario in your mind, let it go, along with the fear. As you let go, visualize a positive outcome.

Not-Accepting-Myself-Now Clutter

Often people keep things that require them to change before they may enjoy the benefits. An example of this would be clothes you hope to fit into someday. This kind of clutter can make you feel as though you are not good enough as you are now. The expression "what you resist persists" applies here. It is better to support and accept who you are now and let go of things that make you feel inadequate.

Collections

Creating a collection can be a meaningful, enjoyable hobby. However, be sure it doesn't take over your home and life. Everything you collect needs a designated place. If the items start to look cluttered and crammed together, or spill over into every part of your home, you will not be able to appreciate or enjoy them. Keep only your favorite things and let go of the rest. Also, be sure that the objects still have as much meaning to you now as they did when you started collecting. If not, then perhaps it is time to make space for something new in your life. Maintaining a collection takes a lot of time—make sure it is time well spent.

Mental Clutter

"Mental clutter" is your personal to-do list, particularly the low priority items that never get put down on paper but weigh heavily on your mind. Have you ever put off replacing a burnt-out lightbulb for weeks? How many times did you think about doing this chore? Every day for weeks and weeks? Each time you think about it you are expending energy. When your personal space is filled with unfinished tasks, your energy is dispersed and depleted. You have less space in your mind to devote to your projects, to be creative, or just to enjoy the moment.

One of the greatest gifts you can give to your child and yourself is to be available in the moment both physically and mentally. It is hard to be present with someone when your mind is scanning an endless to-do list. A great exercise described in David Allen's book *Getting Things Done* is called a "mind sweep." To mind sweep, take twenty minutes to quickly write down all the things that are grabbing your attention, large or small, from picking up the dry cleaning to the screenplay you intend to write one day. Next, organize your list into high priority items, low priority items, tasks that must be done by a specific date, things you know you will do, and things you may choose not to do. You may wish to identify those things on the list that you decide are important to complete before your baby is born. You do not need to complete everything on your list immediately or ever, but decide what action you will take on each item in the future. You might be surprised at just how much mental clutter you carry around. Just the physical act of writing down all the things on your mind will help clear mental clutter that distracts you from the present moment.

Keep this exercise in mind when you're a new parent. There are so many things, particularly in the first few months after your baby is born, that you simply won't have time to do, but seeing these items on paper can help you relax. Most likely you'll find that many things on your list can wait. Once you're spending time with your baby, it's amazing to discover how many things that you used to feel were a high priority can now wait indefinitely. When you have the time, refer to this ongoing list and see what you would actually like to complete.

Unwanted Gifts and Items We Inherit

You have probably received gifts that you don't need or that don't fit your personal taste. Don't feel you have to keep something just to please the person who gave it to you. It truly is the thought that counts, not the material item. So thank the person who gave you the gift and then tactfully either return it to the store or give it to someone who really can use it.

Too Expensive to Let Go Of

Everyone occasionally makes a mistake and buys something only to realize later that it wasn't truly wanted. Forgive yourself for your mistake and let the item go. It is a greater waste of money to just let it sit unused. Either sell it or give it away to someone who will really appreciate it. You are making more space to receive something you will truly value. Don't let guilt facilitate clutter.

Clearing as Meditation

By taking the time a few months before the baby is born to clear away clutter, you are making space for your baby both emotionally and physically. The process of clutter clearing can be very therapeutic and meditative. The rhythm of cleaning can give an active mind a break, and a few days of clutter clearing will often leave you with more clarity, or provide you with a new perspective on your life. Sometimes you may want to let go of an object that is in good condition, or even beautiful, simply because it is no longer "you," or because the object triggers a negative memory or association. By letting go of old "stuff" you can let go of emotional baggage and beliefs that limit your ideas about your life or yourself.

Twelve Steps to Clutter Clearing

1. **Set aside time.** Do not start clutter clearing your kitchen at five o'clock in the evening if you plan to eat at home that night—it might get worse before it gets better.

2. **Be prepared.** You will need separate boxes or bags for recyclables, garbage, giveaways, things you intend to sell, and things that need to be repaired.

3. **Set an intention.** An intention may be to let go of anything that no longer serves you or to create a supportive environment that brings you peace and joy.

4. **Start small.** Go room by room, closet by closet, shelf by shelf, and drawer by drawer. Start with the easiest and perhaps smallest room. Once you've picked a room, stick with it and complete it before moving on to the next room. Begin with one drawer, one shelf, or one cabinet. Successful completion of one area will give you positive reinforcement and motivate you for the more challenging areas.

5. **Take everything out first.** For example, if you start with a closet, first take everything out of the closet. Everything. This step will ensure that you address each item. Otherwise it's too easy to skim the surface, dealing with only a few items, and ignoring the rest.

6. **Clean the empty drawer, shelf, or cabinet before you put things back inside.** A clean and fresh space will inspire you to only put back things that keep it looking good.

7. **Take each item out of the closet and ask yourself the following questions:** Will I use it? Is this item a reflection of who I am now? Is this in alignment with the life I am choosing? Does it support my current goals? Do I love it? Do I need it? If the answer to these questions is no, it is time to let go. Ideally everything in your home will be functional, beautiful, or loved.

8. **Organize the things you are ready to let go of into piles.** Pile 1: Donations. Many companies will pick up donations. You may want to schedule a pickup in advance. Pile 2: Friends and Family. You may have bought something that never quite fit you, just wasn't the right color, but the size or color would be perfect for your friend. Chances are your friend will appreciate it and return the favor. Arrange to give these items to friends and family within a week. Pile 3: Salable Items. Garage sales or the internet are two obvious and easy ways to sell things. If you are never going to use your great-grandmother's china, first offer it to other members of your family. If no one wants it then by all means sell it, but think carefully about whether you really have the time to commit to selling items. Pile 4: Garbage and Recyclables. Take the garbage

bags straight to the trash as soon as they are full. Pile 5: Repairs. Only hold on to things that require repairs (clothes or shoes, for example) if you have the time and resources to fix them soon.

9. **One year rule.** If you can't make a decision about certain items, don't spend hours deliberating. It's important to keep moving throughout this process. Create an undecided box, and pack these items neatly inside and then store the box in an organized space for one year. If you haven't missed these things in a year, let them go. You don't even need to open the box—just give it away.

10. **Put back and organize the keepers.** Take your time. Find a good place for each of your possessions and neatly stack, hang, or fold them, making sure each item is appropriately accessible. Any drawer, closet, or space should be a pleasure to look at. You may wish to organize a closet by color, season, or some personal system that supports your lifestyle and routines.

11. **Go through each room in your house.** Each closet, each drawer, each shelf, until your whole space is completely streamlined. If you start feeling as if there are some things you "need," make a list, but do not buy anything yet. Revisit the list at a later date; you might be surprised to find that you can't remember why it seemed so important to buy these things.

12. **Maintain.** The nice thing about a huge overhaul is that it will last indefinitely with maintenance. Each week go through your home and check for clutter. Make sure that everything is in place, and clear out anything that doesn't belong. This process may be fairly quick; a two-bedroom apartment will take about twenty minutes. This can be a conscious process where you reset intentions for order, simplicity, and peace in your life. Each spring, you may wish to embark on a larger clearing, but if you've maintained throughout the year, it should take much less time than your initial clearing. A good way to maintain equilibrium in terms of volume is to make sure that each time you bring something new into your home you let go of a corresponding item. For example if you buy a new shirt, let go of an old one. It is impossible to create clutter if you follow this simple rule.

A few common challenges:

Photographs and letters. Putting together albums is very time-consuming and should not hold you back from finishing your clutter clearing. Focus on clutter clearing before organization. Complete the clearing process by throwing away letters and pictures that you decide not to keep, and then place the remainder neatly into a container. Ask yourself the following questions: Is this an important part of my family history? Is this a good memory that makes me feel happy? Will my children appreciate or learn from this? (Keep in mind that you do not want to weigh your children down with unnecessary baggage, and if they're old enough, ask them how they feel.) When you consciously choose items to keep and have neatly placed them in the containers, they're no longer clutter. When you have the time, you can pull out the containers and work on your albums.

Making a mistake. Another common reason to hold on to clutter is to compensate for a "mistake" such as buying something costly and then never wearing it, using it, or even liking it. Each time you look at these items you may judge yourself as wasteful or berate yourself for making such a poor choice. If you continue to hold on to this item, the result is that you repeat the "mistake" on two levels: on the physical level, you are continuing to waste the product again and again by not giving it away to someone who may have a use for it; on the metaphysical level, you are judging yourself over and over. The action of buying it is neutral—it is the judgments that make it wrong.

"Free spirit" clutter. Often people will hold on to clutter because they mistakenly equate mess with being a free spirit. You may think being or-ganized and streamlined will rob you of spontaneity. In fact, the opposite is true. If you have an impulse to take an exotic vacation, but you can't find your passport, you have taken away from the spontaneity and freedom of the moment. You may also resist making plans so you can live moment to

An organized changing table with drawers, a hamper, and a caddy ensures you have a place for everything you need within reach.

moment without feeling tied down. Yet, if you do not commit to a plan you will find yourself wasting time wavering about the future. The sooner you are able to make your plans and set a schedule, the sooner you can live in the present moment.

Remember not to wear yourself out. Your first priority is staying healthy, particularly when carrying a baby. Do not expect to simplify your home in a day. You may choose to do one drawer or one shelf a day. Marla Cilley, in her book *Sink Reflections,* suggests clearing clutter in fifteen-minute spurts. She recommends taking fifteen minutes each day to get rid of as much stuff as you possibly can, and then stopping. If you feel overwhelmed by your clutter, try doing this exercise for one month. Even fifteen minutes of clutter clearing is an effective way to shift the energy in your home. When you do decide to carry out the twelve steps described in this chapter, you will already have more energy from the clutter you were able to let go of in the fifteen-minute spurts and you will have less to clear. At the end of the month, it should be very manageable to carry out the Twelve Step Process.

Organization

When you find yourself procrastinating and avoiding certain tasks, such as paying bills, ask yourself if this is because the things you need to pay the bills with, like stamps and envelopes, are not readily available or organized. Anxiety over not knowing where an important document is, or the dread of opening the closet door where things topple out on you, is enough to make you avoid it.

Any time you avoid a small quick task, check to see if it is because of an organizational issue. Would you be more apt to take the trash out regularly if you didn't need to search under the sink for the new bags? Would you put your laundry in a hamper more regularly if it were easily accessible?

Disorganization zaps your time, just as clutter zaps your energy. Everything needs a place in your home where it is readily accessible and can be easily put away, otherwise you will experience clutter again in no time. It is very important that your home supports you once you have a baby. Few things are as frustrating as standing at a changing table with a wiggling baby and a dirty diaper, running out of wipes, and not being able to find the extras. Consider setting up your home so that it's functional and the things you use on a daily basis are easily accessible. This may mean storing things in places not traditionally meant for that purpose. Maybe you never thought to have wipes and diapers in a kitchen drawer, but if it saves you a trip up the stairs carrying your baby it might be worth it. Empower yourself through organization.

Storage

Babies come with a lot of stuff that they outgrow quickly. Decide before your baby is born what you want to do with all these things. Do you want to save them to use for your next child? Do you have a friend or sibling you want to give them to? Keep in mind all you've learned about clutter as you decide what to do. Once you make a decision, be sure you have enough space in your home for everything you plan to save. Keep an area in your garage, your basement, or a closet empty in anticipation of everything you will want to store. Buy storage containers and put them in that area so that when the time comes you're prepared. When you're sleep deprived and caring for a baby, shopping for storage containers may feel like a huge project, so do it now when you have the time. You will be amazed at how quickly babies' items multiply, so having a well-thought-out storage system and planning in advance can be the key to preventing clutter.

If after clutter clearing and organizing your home still feels crowded, lacks storage space, or simply isn't large enough for your growing family, then consider the following suggestions:

1. Set an intention to move to a more appropriately sized space by making a list of everything you are looking for in your next home.

2. Store your belongings in unconventional spaces. For example, re-purpose a dish cabinet that holds formal dishes you use once a year or not at all. Dishes can go in a garage or other remote storage. It is more important to have space for the things you use on a daily basis in your home.

3. Check your room usage. If you have an eat-in kitchen and rarely use your dining room, consider turning your dining area into a playroom.

4. Make sure all your furniture has storage. Don't buy big decorative tables without drawers, shelves, or cabinets. Invest in furniture that serves multiple purposes, such as an ottoman that doubles as a storage chest.

5. Make the most of the storage space you do have by outfitting your closets with floor-to-ceiling shelves, or consulting a closet expert.

6. Find more storage space. As a last resort store your items elsewhere. Consider storing things at a friend or family member's house—just make sure not to push your clutter on them. You can also rent a storage unit. But make sure each item you choose to store is truly something that you want to keep.

If well-organized, even a storage system can be attractive.

Changing Habits That Create Clutter

Once you have a clutter-free, simplified, and organized home, you will most likely want to keep it that way by stopping clutter at the door. The only way to stay clutter-free is to stop accumulating it, and this means changing your habits and thinking differently about what you bring into your home. When you buy something, realize you are investing your time as well as your money. Think of it as if you're beginning a new relationship. Ask yourself the following questions: Do I love it? Do I really need it? Do I have time to take care of it? Alter it? Clean it? Do I have the time to read the directions and learn how to use it? Is it worth it? Do I have a place to keep it where it can be easily retrieved and put back again?

Keep in mind that many of the things our friends and the media tell us that we *must have* to parent our children are completely unnecessary. The essentials alone are overwhelming, so be very discerning as you make your way through all the baby accessories available. Some things may be very helpful and save time, but many things will just get in your way and make you feel more overwhelmed. You don't have to constantly buy new toys to entertain your child. Allow your child to tap into his creativity and imagination and entertain himself. Ask any parent and they will likely tell you that the toys their children like best are usually not the store-bought toys, but everyday household items such as the telephone, a paper towel roll, or mixing bowls. Children are often only excited by new toys for about a week, so avoid the toy frenzy and save yourself time, money, and space. Simply cleaning and reorganizing toys can spark new interest.

Keep this in mind when registering for baby gifts. Friends and family are usually very generous when a baby is born. Registering is a way of making sure their time and energy is well spent. Some people don't know to ask if you are registered or may already have a gift in mind, but chances are you won't need everything you receive so plan on returning things. For items you cannot return, don't feel badly about giving them away to someone who can truly use and appreciate them. If anyone should ask you what you would like, and you already have the essentials, consider asking for a home-cooked meal after the baby is born, a gift certificate, or babysitting.

Teaching Your Children to Clear Clutter

Children need space and quiet time. When you create this space in their outer environment, you help nurture and cultivate their sense of inner peace. Allow your baby room to grow by leaving empty space for new things. The best way to teach children to take responsibility for their environment is to set an example. When they see you picking up, recycling, giving things away, and caring for your home, they will learn to do the same. As children get older they may even become active participants in the clutter-clearing process. Children will learn that it is safe to let things go and they can trust that all their needs will be met as more appropriate things come into their lives.

Involving children in the process of taking care of their toys and clutter clearing will help you when it comes time to explain why you are not going to buy them a new toy every time you visit a store. You can teach your children to decide what toys and clothes they would like to keep, throw away, or donate. You can even help them choose an organization to donate to. If your young child has a toy that he doesn't play with, but is hesitant to part with, consider temporarily "toy swapping" with another friend. This is a great way to make space and let them play with "new" things. Another option is to rotate the toys. Keep half of the toys stored in a closet and the other half available, and then periodically rotate them. This way, on a daily basis, you will only need to take care of half of the volume. In fact, you might find that you have a helper sooner than you might expect. Children love putting toys away into containers and chests.

Quick Tips

• Simplify. Clear your space of things that do not represent your dreams or empower you to fulfill your goals. Ask yourself the following questions: Does this object reflect who I am now in my life? Does it support my current goals? Do I need it? (Is it useful?) Do I love it? You should be able to answer yes to at least one of the above questions for every item in your home. If your answer is no to all of the above questions, consider selling the object, giving it away, or throwing it away. If you do not love something it is better to live without it (unless it is very functional).

• Surround yourself with beautiful things that you enjoy and that inspire you. Make sure that you love at least one thing in each room of your home. If it's not there already, find a cherished object or beautiful plant to place in that room.

• Eliminate mental clutter by taking a few minutes to write down all the things that are weighing on your mind. Then organize this list into high priority items, such as things that must be done by a specific date, and things you may or may not ever do. Just the act of writing down all the things on your mind helps clear mental clutter.

• Organize. Find a "home" for your stuff. Everything needs a place where it is readily accessible and can be easily put away, or you will feel cluttered again in no time.

• Buy storage containers. Before your baby is born, decide what you want to do with all the things that the baby outgrows. Do you want to save it to use for your next child? Do you have a friend or sibling you want to give it to? Once you make a decision be sure you have enough space and storage in your home for everything you plan to keep.

Chapter Three

Preparing the Room

Now it is time to turn your attention to the nursery. This chapter focuses on all the things you can do to prepare the room before bringing in furniture and decorative elements. Cleaning and painting the room are essential beginning steps toward creating a fresh environment for you and your baby. As you take these initial steps toward creating a nursery, keep in mind that each effort and act of making a special space for your child is a gift, particularly if you fill the process with loving and positive thoughts.

Choosing a Room

You may or may not have a choice of rooms for your nursery, but any space prepared with love and good intentions will envelop your baby with positive energy. You can create nurturing surroundings for your baby in almost any type of space: a nook, alcove, large room, small room, or shared room.

If you are going to set up the nursery in your bedroom, a sibling's bedroom, or a room that serves another function, such as a guest room or office, try to separate the nursery from the rest of the room as much as possible. You can use curtains, screens, or large pieces of furniture to enclose the baby's space and create a sense of privacy. Dividing the space is particularly important if your baby will be sharing a room with a sibling. Ideally children will have a space they can call their own, such as a bed and a nightstand or their own dresser. Consider defining each child's space with small area rugs and with bed linens that are different from one another, yet complementary.

If you do have a choice of rooms, there are several guidelines to help you choose a room with calm and protective energy. Keep these guidelines in mind when you make your decision, but also trust your instincts. A particular room may feel right to you because it is closer to your bedroom, because it gets great sunlight, or because it just feels good. If you picture yourself with your baby in a certain room, and the room seems to call out to you, then this space is most likely the perfect place for your baby.

If possible, all bedrooms should be placed in the back or middle of the house. Rooms located toward the back of the house have a peaceful energy and are more conducive to sleep. Rooms located in the front of the house are subject to the activity of the front door and have a more lively energy. This guideline is especially relevant if your house is located close to a busy street. Streets have very active energy and their bright lights and loud noises can disrupt a good night's sleep.

However, if your nursery is located near a busy street, don't worry; you can still create a restful sanctuary. Hang blackout curtains or shades to eliminate streetlights and consider installing double pane windows to block out noise. A less expensive option is to purchase a white noise machine to mask unwanted sounds.

When considering the placement of the nursery also bear in mind that in Feng Shui, parents' bedrooms should ideally be located in one of the back corners of the house, kitty-corner to the front door of the home, which is referred to as the Command Position (see Diagram 3A). The Command Position, also known as the Power Position, is used to describe the place in a room or home where a person will feel the most protected and empowered. The master bedroom is best located in the Command Position of a house; you are more empowered in the Command Position because everything in your home is stretched out before you. Even though you can't see through walls, symbolically you have a full view of everything happening in your home and life. The back left corner of a house is particularly powerful because it is associated with a family's prosperity and therefore is an even stronger Power Position than the back right corner.

Children's rooms should ideally be located in the middle of the home. When children's rooms are located in the Command Position, the sense that their needs rule the family often follows. However, if a smaller child's room is located in the Command Position and a larger master bedroom suite is not, it is still better for parents to choose the larger room. To restore a sense of balance in this situation, place a photograph of you and your spouse in the Command Position of your child's room (see Diagram 4A, page 60), preferably one that is larger than any photographs of your child that are also in the room.

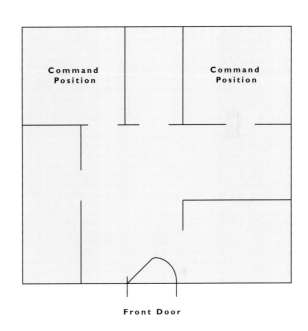

Diagram 3A

The rooms in the back of the house across from the front door are considered to be in the Command Position because even though you can't see through walls, symbolically you have a "view" of everything happening in your home.

Try to avoid placing the nursery over the garage; it's difficult to feel grounded with the unstable energy and noise created by the coming and going of cars beneath you. If you must place the nursery over the garage, you can create a sense of stability by grounding the room with a square or rectangular rug and anchoring the energy with a few heavy pieces of furniture. It is also a good idea to install a carbon monoxide detector.

Renovations and Repairs

After you choose the room, take a moment to list anything that needs to be repaired. Determine if there are any changes that you'd like to make, or if you anticipate any small renovations. Going through a renovation is almost always

disruptive and challenging, and is even more so for a new parent. You will want your first year with your baby to be as peaceful as possible.

If you anticipate any modest renovations in the next few years, and your budget permits, it's best to complete them before the baby is born. An appropriate project might be outfitting a closet with built-ins: babies' things seem to multiply and the more space you have for them to grow into the better. It is unadvisable to make any major renovations while you are pregnant, such as tearing down walls or scraping paint, because you don't want to risk exposing yourself to the harmful toxins

The white walls are balanced by lively red accents.

and dust that renovations can agitate. In general, pregnancy is not a time to take on big projects, as your energy should be reserved for your nine-month project of creating a human life.

Anything that is broken interrupts the ease in which you perform your daily routines and can disrupt the flow of energy in a space. Negotiating with a stuck drawer each morning is not a supportive way to start the day. Additionally, each time you walk by and see a broken object that needs to be repaired or replaced, your energy is depleted as this task weighs on your mind. So if you need to make any repairs to the room—such as doors that creak or do not close properly, broken doorknobs, leaky faucets, cracked windowpanes, or faulty outlets—do so before your baby is born. Imagine the frustration you would feel after finally getting your baby to sleep, and then as you are tiptoeing out of the nursery to enjoy your personal time, the door creaks, startling and waking your sleeping baby.

Color

Once you have selected the room, empty it of all its contents so you may begin with a fresh canvas. Sit in the room and imagine being there with your baby. What colors come to mind? Don't feel restricted by the traditional color palettes of pink for a girl's nursery and blue for a boy's nursery. Let your mind wander. How do these colors make you feel? When your child grows older you can respond to his or her taste; in the meantime, it is important that *you* feel good in the room, as your baby will pick up on how you feel. Remember that you will be spending almost as much time in this room as your baby, so it is important that you like the color too.

Perhaps now you have a few colors in mind. If so, remember your choices as this next section discusses the effect different colors have on your mind and body. Color is created by wavelengths of light; each wavelength produces a unique vibration and energy that can affect your mood. Today, it is widely accepted that different colors produce different emotional responses. You can see this link between color and mood in your day-to-day life. You probably feel different when wearing a bright yellow sweater than you feel dressed in all black. Frequently expressions are used that connect emotions to different colors such as "feeling blue," "seeing red," or "being green with envy."

Overall, soothing colors, such as pastels, will be the best choice for a nursery. However, if you are drawn to a bright color like red, try selecting a lighter, less active shade of that color such as a deep pink, or use it as an accent by adding red toys, pillows, blankets, or artwork that incorporates splashes of red. If you still aren't particularly drawn to any one color then use the different effects of color as a guide.

Things to Consider When Choosing a Color

- **Blue** encourages relaxation and is therefore an excellent color for bedrooms. It is often linked with peace, healing, and meditation. A light blue bedroom is particularly good for inducing sleep and so it can be a perfect choice for the nursery.

- **Red** is a very active color and is often associated with passion, power, and in some cultures, good luck. Although it is too active and overpowering for nursery walls, red can combat lethargy. Red is appropriate in small doses and will boost your energy.

- **Pink** is the color of love, both self-love and love for others. A soft pink may be a very nice choice for the baby's room.

- **Green** is the color most associated with nature and therefore represents both serenity and growth. It has the potential both to calm and revitalize. If you live in an urban environment, adding green to your nursery can be an excellent way to connect to nature. A soft, spring green can be a wonderful choice for the nursery.

- **Yellow** is the color associated with the sun. Yellow sheds light on our lives and helps us see things clearly. It is an excellent color to promote clarity.

Yellow can also be a good choice for a nursery because it is uplifting. Bright yellow is energizing, however, so choose a pale shade that will not interfere with sleep.

- **Purple** may be a calming, reassuring color but it is also very stimulating. Purple is associated with spirituality as well as royalty. If you are drawn to purple, you may wish to use **lavender** in your nursery. Lavender, like blue, promotes relaxation and therefore may help soothe your baby.

- **Orange** is a very happy and expansive color. Although perhaps too active a color in a room used for sleep, it can make an excellent accent color.

- **White** is a very clean color and works in all rooms. White is associated with purity. However, since it can look sterile, you may wish to accent it with warmer colors. Alternatively, try **off-white**, which has some yellow in it to bring in the sunshine energy; or **beige**, which is still very neutral and yet much warmer.

- **Black** is associated with the unconscious. Black is a creative and powerful color, but would be oppressive in a nursery, so only use it in small doses.

Paint

Now that you have selected a color you must choose your brand of paint. Be aware that many paints give off toxic fumes known as volatile organic compounds (VOCs), which can be harmful to you and your child. These chemicals can remain in the air even after the paint is dry. Low- or no-VOC paints are a healthier alternative to this problem and can now be found almost anywhere in the United States. (See Resources.) Even if you use a low- or no-VOC paint, you will want to paint your nursery at least a month in advance of when your baby arrives and keep the windows open, so that the majority of remaining VOCs and other solvents will have time to dissipate beforehand. Natural paints, such as milk paint, are also a healthier choice. Pregnant women should avoid painting the room altogether.

If your home was built before 1978, or if the paint in your house is cracking, chipping, or peeling, or if you are renovating, you may want to have a professional test for lead paint, which can be hazardous to your child's health. For more information, visit the U.S. Environmental Protection Agency website at www.epa.gov or call the National Lead Information Center at 1-800-424-LEAD (5323). If you contact your local health department, you may be able to have lead paint testing done free of charge. Otherwise, the Lead Information Center will put you in touch with HUD Lead Listing for a certified specialist in your area.

Floors and Lighting

Wall-to-wall carpeting can trap pollutants, mold, and dust mites, which can trigger allergies and asthma. Synthetic carpeting is treated with chemicals such as stain repellants and flame-retardants, and glued down with adhesives that contain VOCs, which can release fumes for up to five years. While wool is naturally dust mite and bacteria resistant it can be difficult to find wool carpets that have not been treated with chemicals. Therefore it is best to avoid wall-to-wall carpeting. If hardwood floors are underneath your wall-to-wall carpeting, remove the carpeting and opt for area rugs in natural, untreated fibers. If you are pregnant be sure to have someone else remove the carpets and clean the floor. If you don't have (and don't want to install) hardwood floors, another natural option is cork flooring, which is a soft yet firm surface where your baby can learn to crawl and walk. You could also install ceramic tile, bamboo, or natural linoleum and soften the surface with natural fiber, untreated area rugs. Choose smaller area rugs that can be easily cleaned. Between milk stains and leaking diapers you can expect to clean your rug more than once. For area rugs that are not machine washable you can spot clean with natural cleaners and then place them outside in the sunlight, which will help eliminate dust mites.

If you decide to keep wall-to-wall carpeting, it will be especially important to vacuum frequently. The best vacuums contain a High Efficiency Particulate Air (HEPA) filter to remove dust particles. It will also help to have people remove their shoes indoors so pollutants do not get trapped in the carpet. If your wall-to-wall carpeting is in good condition, you might want to keep it rather than risk exposing yourself to the VOCs that a new carpet will release into the air. If you need to replace your carpet, try to be out of the house while the new carpet is being installed and keep the windows open for several days. (For more information about additional healthy guidelines for choosing, installing, and maintaining wall-to-wall carpeting, visit the Children's Health Environmental Coalition website, checnet.org.)

The most comfortable rooms in a home usually employ a variety of lighting options: natural, overhead, and task lighting. In the nursery, you will want some overhead lighting because your baby will be walking before you know it and you may need to remove floor lamps that the baby can (and will) knock over.

Ideally the nursery will have the perfect balance of natural sunlight, not too bright and not too dark. Sunlight not only provides us with vitamin D, an essential nutrient, it also supports our emotional health. In the summer months when we are exposed to more daylight we tend to feel lighter, happier, and more energized. Winter is often a time when it is difficult to get out of bed and motivate. Natural sunlight also connects us to nature and helps our bodies recognize day and night and prepare for sleep and awake times.

Newborns are particularly sensitive to light, so you'll want to be able to adjust both the natural and artificial light in the baby's nursery. If the room gets too much bright sun, consider installing sheer cloth panels for filtering daytime light beneath heavier curtains for naps and bedtime. If the room requires using a lot of artificial light, and you don't have dimmer switches, you can place a few table lamps with low wattages around the room so you can adjust the light depending on the situation.

It is wonderful when a nursery has windows, both for the natural sunlight and the fresh air they provide. However, a room with too many windows can also become drafty. Newborns are extremely sensitive to temperature, so if the baby's room has a lot of windows, you might need to add extra weather stripping to keep the temperature at a consistent sixty-seven to seventy degrees.

Cleaning

A common and essential aspect of caring for our homes is removing dust and dirt, which, over time, can negatively affect our physical health and dampen our spirits. A thorough cleaning can transform the energy in a room. Give your baby a fresh start by cleaning the nursery room from top to bottom.

Many household cleaning products contain chemicals such as ammonia and phenol, which can irritate your skin and lungs, and can cause headaches. Household cleaning products, air fresheners and dry cleaning can cause indoor air pollution. To avoid exposing yourself and your baby to these hazardous pollutants, open windows to freshen your home, air out dry cleaning before putting it in your closet, and look for nontoxic, environmentally safe household cleaning products. There is now a wide range of all-natural cleaning products available in stores; they are gentler on our bodies, as well as to the environment, and are still extremely effective cleaners. (See Resources.) Many of these products contain essential oils, so you can enjoy the smell of lavender, basil, orange, or lemon as you clean. If you have the time, you can also make your own cleaning products (see Sidebar below). Further information on how to make your own cleaning products can be found in Annie Berthold-Bond's book *Clean and Green*.

Windows: Mix ¼ cup vinegar with 2 cups water in a spray bottle. Shake before use.

Wood surfaces and floors: Mix ¼ cup vinegar to a gallon of water with a few drops of lemon essential oil.

Scouring powder: Sprinkle baking soda on surface and scrub with a damp sponge.

Walls: Add Castille liquid soap to a gallon of water.

Energy Cleansing

Just as essential as cleaning away dust and dirt is clearing away stagnant and unhelpful energy. For thousands of years many cultures have used various techniques to cleanse spaces of negative energy, followed by rituals designed to usher in beneficial energy. Native Americans would burn bundles of herbs, called "smudge sticks," to rid living spaces of negative energy, and then invite in positive spirits with the beat of a drum. The Chinese would chant and beat gongs, while in Bali burning incense is a daily practice. In churches, salt and incense are still common tools used to protect and consecrate spaces. Today it is common to create sacred space through such simple acts as lighting candles before a wedding or religious ceremony.

Your home is alive with energy. Even though people can't see the energy moving, they can often sense it. Have you ever walked into a room after others have been in a fight and sensed the hostility in the air? You didn't hear or see the argument, but you could "cut the tension with a knife"? What you are sensing is stagnant energy in the air. In this context, the expression "we need to clear the air" takes on new meaning. You may have had the experience of walking into a room that may be beautifully decorated, but somehow just doesn't feel right. Or perhaps you walk into a space that may not reflect your personal taste, but you immediately feel good. In both these instances, you are tuning in to the energy in the room.

Each room in your home holds the energy of every person who has ever entered the room and every event that took place there. When the flow of energy in a room is blocked, events and emotions build up over time. Although some of the people and events may hold positive energy, others may hold negative energy. Over time, this energy collects, builds up, and stagnates. Babies are sensitive to different energies, so it is important to give your baby a new beginning by cleansing and moving stagnant energy.

An Energy Cleansing is a simple process that you can use to create a free flow of healthy, vibrant energy. There are many "tools" you can use to cleanse a room (see Sidebar). You may use an atomizer filled with water and essential oils to mist the room, or burn incense to smoke the room. Certain essential oils should not be used by pregnant women and incense should be used in moderation and with care. If you are sensitive or allergic to essential oils or smoke, you can use sound instead to cleanse the room. Either "clap" the room by walking around the room clapping your hands to break up stagnant energy, or "tone" the room by ringing a bell and letting the tone resonate. Or to create a soothing atmosphere fitting for the nursery, use a flower dipped in water to flick water around the room to break up old energy. By using a flower as a tool you replace stagnant energy with the gentle energy of that flower. Whichever method you choose, keep in mind that the most important aspect of a cleansing is your intention.

Energy Cleansing Tools:

Choose the tool that you feel is appropriate for the room.

Smoke: Light sandalwood incense or a sage bundle and wave the smoke around the room. Make sure that no one in your home is allergic or sensitive to smoke. Check the room for a few hours after the cleansing to make sure there are no embers.

Your hands: You may clap your hands around the room to break up the energy.

A bell: Use sound by ringing the bell in different corners of the room and letting the tone resonate, dispersing and clearing the stuck energy.

Essential oils: Add a few drops of lemon essential oil to a mister bottle of water and mist the room.

Flower: Fill a bowl with mineral water and use a flower, such as a pink rose, to "flick" the water around the room. Using a gentle tool like a flower will create a gentle energy.

*Any one of these Energy Cleansing tools
can be used to refresh a room.*

The following is a step-by-step Energy Cleansing ritual:

(Additional information on Energy Cleansings and blessings can be found in Denise Linn's book *Space Clearing A–Z.*)

1. Physically clean the space first and then choose a sunny day to cleanse the energy in the room.

2. Have your Energy Cleansing tool ready.

3. You may wish to ask for assistance from your higher self, spirit, the universe, or any guides or angels.

4. State your intention to release any stagnant energy that may be in the room. Ask that the room be cleared of anything that is not in alignment with optimal health, love, joy, and peace.

5. Begin walking around the room using your Energy Cleansing tool to remove any stagnant energy. Pay particular attention to doorframes, baseboards, and corners. Open any drawers, and closet or cabinet doors. If you have any furniture in the room, cleanse the furniture as well.

6. You may wish to repeat out loud, "This room is now cleansed and purified in preparation for my baby's arrival."

7. After you have finished walking around the room, open the windows so that the stagnant energy can exit the room.

8. Know your Energy Cleansing is complete and successful. Give thanks.

9. Wash your hands.

Blessing

Now that the room's energy is refreshed you may complete this process with a blessing. This is your chance to fill the room energetically with as much loving, positive energy as possible.

1. Open all the windows with the intention of ushering in positive energy.

2. Ask that the room be filled with light, love, blessings, peace, optimal health, and any other quality you desire for your family and baby.

3. Prepare a gift for the room. This offering may be as simple as lighting a candle and placing a vase of fresh flowers in the center of the room. You

may wish to add other symbols of your hopes and dreams for your child by placing them in the room at this time.

You have now given your baby a fresh start. You have honored and blessed the space and now your baby will be nourished by the warm, positive energy. In truth, every moment you take to set up this room for your baby is a blessing.

Quick Tips

• If you have a choice, locate your nursery toward the middle or back of the house.

• Choose soft, pastel paint colors for your walls and reserve the stronger vibrant colors for accents.

• Check for lead and asbestos. Consider removing wall-to-wall carpeting and opt for washable area rugs. Use no- or low-VOC paints and thoroughly clean the room with all-natural cleaning products. If the nursery is located above or next to a garage, install a carbon monoxide detector.

• In addition to physically cleansing the room, also perform an energy cleansing and blessing.

Chapter Four

Comfort and Safety

An environment that is safe and comfortable is essential to our well-being. Never is this truer than when creating a room for a baby. When it comes to interior design, people sometimes choose appearance over comfort and even safety; for example, a formal living room that is beautiful to behold, but where no one in your family ever likes to spend time; or sharp-edged furniture that can be dangerous to both children and adults. Like all new parents, you will want to create a beautiful room for your baby, but before you decide how you'll decorate, you should consider comfort and safety.

Safety

In order to be comfortable, you must first know that you're safe and protected from danger. There are two kinds of danger that can affect your sense of safety—actual and perceived. Actual danger that can cause you physical harm is probably what you imagine when you hear the word danger. To protect your baby from actual danger, you will need to baby-proof your home at some point between birth and when your baby learns to crawl. You can do the baby-proofing yourself or you can hire a professional to take care of the basics, such as covering electrical outlets, securing heavy furniture, installing window guards, locking kitchen drawers, locking toilet lids, securing cords for blinds and curtains, installing smoke and carbon monoxide detectors, and putting up gates in front of stairwells. These are all practical ways to reduce the threat of actual danger.

Perceived danger is more abstract. Perceived danger is anything in your environment that causes you discomfort because it appears dangerous. For example, imagine sitting at a table with a sharp knife pointing directly at you. Although you know that a knife lying motionless on a table cannot harm you, you would most likely prefer not to sit with it pointing at you and would probably either remove it or change seats. In this situation you know that you're not in actual danger, but you perceive danger and therefore feel uncomfortable. Sometimes your sense of logic may override your discomfort and you'll ignore the perceived threat, but remember that before you have time to reason with yourself, your body and mind have already registered the threat and experienced some level of discomfort and stress. In order for your nervous system to relax fully, it is important to remove or mitigate perceived dangers in your living space.

Every home is full of perceived dangers that people tend to ignore or, over time, come to accept. A heavy piece of artwork hanging above a bed is a good example: although the chance that the artwork will fall on you while you sleep is slim, the perceived danger might make you feel uncomfortable. Your intellect may override your feelings, but the nagging discomfort remains. To feel fully relaxed and stress-free you must remove or alter the things in your environment that could be perceived as dangerous—and nowhere does this apply more than in the nursery. Your baby's room should help her feel as secure and comfortable as possible.

Common perceived dangers include anything heavy hanging directly above your baby's head as he sleeps, such as mobiles, art, and ceiling fans. Although a mobile can be entertaining by daylight, imagine the uncomfortable feeling of waking up in the middle of the night and having an object looming over you. Like the heavy artwork hanging above the headboard of your bed, the mobile is a perceived threat and should be removed or pushed aside during the night. Sharp or protruding corners created by walls that extend into the room, or square and rectangular furniture with sharp edges and corners are also considered perceived dangers in Feng Shui. Sharp angles, when pointing toward an area where you and your child spend a lot of time, such as the nursing chair or the crib, can cause you both discomfort. Check your baby's room for anything that you feel may be sending out sharp energy. A corner on a wooden table may feel less threatening than a corner on a metal or glass table. You may want to remove furniture with sharp edges; walls with a pointed edge can be softened by simply placing a plant, a lamp, or a piece of furniture in front of the corner.

As you prepare for the arrival of your baby, you will begin looking at your home in a whole new way. Keep in mind that the things that make you feel most safe and comfortable probably have the same effect on your baby.

Healthy Nursery

Another aspect of safety is creating a healthy environment for you and your baby. Surprisingly, many common products used to decorate the nursery, including certain types of paint, finishes, carpeting, mattresses, curtains, particleboard, and cleaning products, contain chemicals. Many of the chemicals used in manufacturing these products, such as formaldehyde, toluene, and benzene, are volatile organic compounds (VOCs) that, through a process called "off-gassing," release fumes into the air, causing harmful indoor air pollution. Because of the small size of their still immature lungs, infants are even more vulnerable than adults to the ill effects of these chemicals. Furthermore, babies tend to play on the floor where dust and airborne chemicals settle. New furniture and fresh paint off-gas at a higher rate than older furniture and paint, so by preparing a nursery with a fresh coat of paint and new baby furniture, parents are unintentionally polluting the air their baby will breathe.

The ideal approach to creating a healthy home and nursery is to first identify any materials that contain harmful toxins, such as synthetic carpets, lead paint, pressed wood, and certain cleaning products, and then seal or remove those materials from your environment. The next step is to replace unhealthy materials with organic or natural alternatives. New pollutants enter our homes on an ongoing basis, and it is difficult to remove all toxins from an environment; therefore, a third step could be to add a HEPA/carbon filter to your heating,

A solid wood crib, wool area rug, and hardwood floors
are beautiful and healthy choices for the nursery.

ventilation, and air conditioning systems, or place standing filters in the nursery and bedrooms to filter the air in your home.

Fortunately, there are also a number of simple solutions to help you create a healthy home and nursery. Simply opening your windows to ventilate your home on a regular basis will reduce indoor air pollution. A study by the Environmental Protection Agency found that pollution inside a home could be two to five times higher than outside the home, even in large, industrialized cities (for more information, visit the EPA website, epa.gov). Opening windows creates a path for chemicals released from common household items to exit and for fresh air to enter. Even opening your windows for ten minutes a day can make a difference. One very effective quick fix for the nursery is to paint and buy nursery furniture a few months before your baby is due and then leave the nursery windows open as often as possible to ventilate the room—a large percentage of VOCs will off-gas in the first few months. Another simple solution is to have people remove their shoes before they enter your home. In this way, pesticides from lawn and garden products, pollutants and dirt will not be tracked inside your home. Since chemicals can bind to house dust, keeping your home free of dust by cleaning regularly with a damp cloth or mop is yet another simple way to make your home healthier.

Healthy Furniture

To keep prices lower, many furniture manufacturers use MDF, plywood, and particleboard when making furniture for babies and children. These materials contain chemicals, such as formaldehyde, and can give off toxic fumes for years. Ideally you want to find furniture made of solid wood, wicker, or rattan. If you have a choice of finish, select low-VOC, water-based products or use natural oil and wax finishes.

If you do purchase furniture made in non-natural materials, or if your furniture is treated with a finish or wood sealer that contains chemicals, place the furniture outside or in a ventilated garage for at least a month before you use it so that some of the fumes can off-gas. If you don't have an outdoor space, place the new furniture in the nursery and keep the windows open and the air circulating for at least a month. Painted or finished furniture will release the majority of fumes in the first few months, and fortunately off-gas more quickly (unlike particleboard and plywood which, unless sealed, can release trace amounts of fumes for years).

Used furniture more than five years old has most likely off-gassed any harmful chemicals, which makes buying or borrowing used furniture an excellent way to be health conscious, stay within a small budget, and practice recycling. However, you might not want to use a hand-me-down crib, as it may not meet current safety standards (for more information about antique crib safety, visit the National Safety Council website, nsc.org). Hand-me-down cribs might also be painted with lead paint, which was not banned until 1978. Since babies often suck on whatever they can get their mouths on, including crib bars, don't use a painted crib unless you are certain it is not painted with lead paint.

Comfortable Furniture

Choose furniture that is comfortable! This sounds obvious, but these days people often buy furniture without seeing it in person. Be sure to give furniture a "test drive" by visiting the store, sitting in chairs, and lying down on beds. Pay

A sofa and oversized armchair make this nursery a comfortable and cozy place to enjoy with your baby.

particular attention to places where you and your baby will spend a good deal of time, especially the chair you plan to use for nursing. Make sure this chair provides the proper back support and comfort you need during feedings. Also keep your child's comfort in mind. As your child learns to sit in a chair, it's best to use furnishings sized to fit children. Consider a small desk and chair where he can comfortably eat, draw, read, or play. This way your child will be comfortable and also gain the confidence and self-esteem that comes from being able to do things without the assistance needed to get in and out of an adult-size piece of furniture.

Select furniture with rounded edges. Pointed edges can cause bruises or even serious harm to a young child who may topple into an edge while learning to crawl, stand, or walk. Sharp edges also look threatening, especially to children at eye level to a coffee table or shelf. Rounded edges look and feel softer and give your baby a sense of comfort.

Furniture Placement

How your furniture is arranged also affects your comfort and safety. Position the nursery furniture in a Command Position so that you and your child have a view of the door (without being directly in front of the door) and a solid wall behind your back (see Diagram 4A). No matter how secure your surroundings are, it's human nature to feel more protected if you have a solid wall behind you, and therefore you may relax knowing that you cannot be surprised from behind. Although we know that it's unlikely that someone will approach us from behind and harm us, our survival instincts prohibit us from feeling fully relaxed unless we are in a position where we can see who or what is coming toward us.

A Command Position is also empowering for two other reasons. First, it allows you to concentrate and focus more fully without being distracted by what is happening behind you, and, second, this position metaphorically symbolizes facing your opportunities. Beds, desks, and sofas are best placed in a Command Position of a room.

Since obviously not all your furniture placement can be in a Command Position, choose the furniture where you and your baby spend the most time, such as the chair where you plan to nurse, and the crib (see Diagram 4B). Place at least one side of the crib against a solid wall so your baby feels secure. By the time your baby is four months old, he will be able to see across the room, so if possible give him a view of the door. Your baby will be more relaxed if he can see who is approaching.

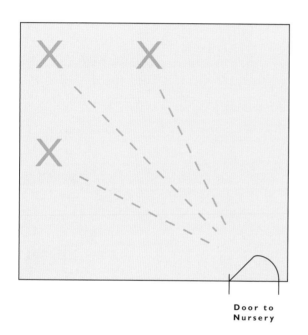

Diagram 4A

There are three locations in this room that are in a Command Position. All of these positions offer a view of the door without being in the path of the door.

Door to Nursery

Avoid placing the crib directly under a window: babies need the support and comfort of a solid wall behind them. In addition to being potentially drafty, having a crib under a window can also be dangerous: cords from curtains and blinds are hazardous, and when your baby gets older and learns to open windows there is a risk that he could fall out. Try not to have the crib near an electrical outlet or any appliances that are always on, such as a digital clock or baby monitor. Electrical outlets and electronics generate electric and magnetic fields

(EMFs), which can potentially cause health problems. While the studies about the effects of EMFs are ongoing, it is wise to avoid the risk. Fortunately, EMFs decline rapidly the farther away you are from the source of electricity, so moving the monitor across the room or repositioning the crib six feet away from an outlet should significantly reduce the effect of EMFs. (For more information about EMFs, visit the Institute for Bau-Biologie and Ecology website, bau-biologieusa.com).

Diagram 4B

In this room, the crib and the nursing chair have a good view of the door to the nursery and are therefore in Command Positions. Ideally, the crib is positioned against a solid wall.

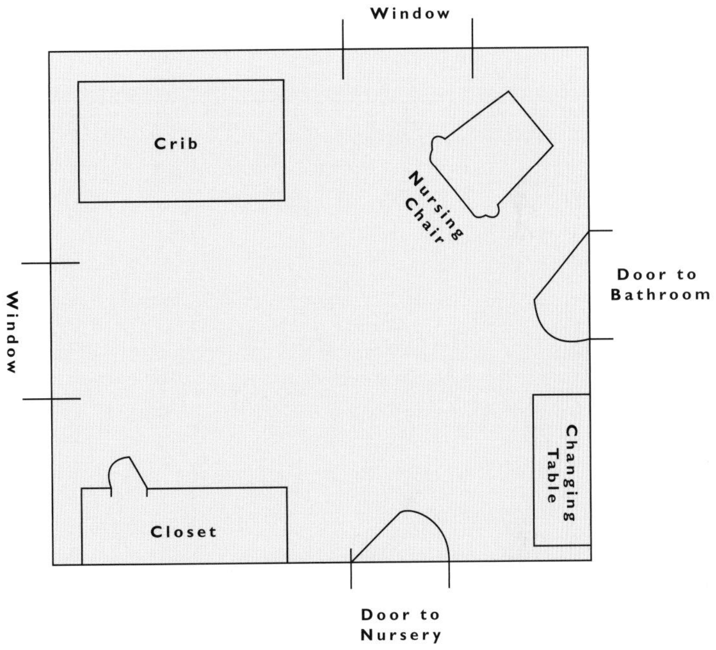

Window

Crib

Nursing Chair

Window

Door to Bathroom

Changing Table

Closet

Door to Nursery

Your Comfort Zone

A comfortable home is a home that supports your lifestyle. Do you prefer a casual environment where everyone congregates in the kitchen or family room, or do you prefer the quiet elegance of a formal living room? Do you like to entertain or spend your weekends alone? Do you enjoy hosting out-of-town guests, or do you value your private space? Be as honest as you can as you answer these questions. Often we are influenced by what we think our lifestyle *should* be or by how we were brought up. The best way to make a home comfortable is for it to reflect who you are now and to serve your unique lifestyle.

Begin by looking at how you use your rooms. Now that another person will be sharing your home, it is especially important to maximize your space. Often people design their homes around events that occur a few times a year, such as holidays, or having guests, even if it's a rare occurrence. You will be most comfortable when your home is designed to function well for you on a daily basis. If you prefer casual get-togethers, perhaps your formal living room is better used as a casual family room. If you rarely have out-of-town guests, or prefer not to, maybe your guest room is better used as a home office. If you never use your formal dining room, consider turning it into a playroom. How you use your rooms is a key element to feeling comfortable in your home. Turning an unused room into something functional can give you the feeling of having added square footage to your home without the cost or time of construction.

Arrange your space in a way that honors your personal preferences and still makes room for your baby. Babies will want to explore all over and touch everything. It's difficult to feel comfortable in your home when you're constantly jumping off the couch to prevent your child from harming himself or damaging something valuable in your home. If you love your collection of glass objects, you will still want them on display, but perhaps now move them from a low table to a high shelf where they will be safe. Seeing cherished objects or expensive fabrics constantly on the brink of being broken or ruined is stressful. You want to relax and unwind in your own home, not live on the edge.

Think about whether you would like to "make space" for your baby in all rooms of your home, or if you prefer to keep some rooms off-limits for playing. Having your children's toys in every room of your house can lead to the feeling that your children are running your home. You may want to have at least one room that is an "adult" room reserved for you and your partner—this could be an office, den, living room, or your bedroom. If you want to feel comfortable with your baby in all areas of your home, prepare the rooms accordingly. One great way to let your child explore is to cover your furniture in washable slipcovers, which will allow you to be comfortable knowing that the jelly fingers reaching for the sofa won't mean re-upholstering your couch. Of course you'll want to teach your child about respecting your house and other people's homes (where there may not be slipcovers), but it's easier to be patient with their learning curve when you are not worried about expensive mistakes.

You may also consider creating a "safe" room in your home that has been thoroughly baby-proofed and is designed for your child to explore. After a long day of being with your child, it can be a real lifesaver if both of you can "play" in the same room for an hour. As your child entertains herself, you can read a book, pay bills, talk on the phone, or just relax knowing that you don't have to be on guard. Another option is to create an area that can be gated off, where your child will be safe, while you do other things (such as, for instance, taking a shower). It is especially helpful to create a baby-proofed area near the kitchen: it can take twice as long to clear a table or make a meal if you're constantly darting in and out of the room to check on your baby.

It's the little things in the back of our minds that unnerve us. Walking into a room with your child and immediately thinking about the lamp he could knock over or the sharp-edged glass coffee table he could bump into is stressful, particularly if you walk into that room ten times a day. Following your child around to keep him out of harm's way is exhausting. If you're a person

Creating a safe play area in a room where you spend a lot of time allows you to keep an eye on your child while you get things done.

who worries a great deal, it can be especially comforting knowing your environment is safe *for* your child as well as safe *from* your child. However, no matter how safe your home is, part of being a parent is always staying tuned in and keeping one eye on your child. It's widely known that children have a gift for finding the one dangerous thing in a room. All the more reason to change whatever you can now.

Energy Flow

In Feng Shui creating balanced energy flow is an important component to comfort. One easy way to see how energy flows in a space is to pay attention to how your eye takes in a room. Wherever your gaze is drawn is where the energy is moving. When energy is flowing smoothly, your gaze will be gently drawn from one area of the room to another, not darting too quickly through the space or getting stuck on one object. Just as it is essential to your well-being that clean air flows freely through your lungs, so too is it vital to the health of your home that the energy circulates freely. In order to keep the energy fresh and uplifted there must be proper circulation and flow. People are most comfortable when the energy in their homes flows in a gentle, meandering way, like a river. So make sure that you can easily move through rooms and avoid placing heavy furniture or objects in your path: if there is an obstruction in your path, the energy will be blocked.

The following list describes places where the flow of energy can be extreme, too fast or too slow:

Staircases: Energy can rush too quickly down staircases. To slow the energy, you could place a small mirror at the bottom of the stairs to "bounce" the energy back up. You could also create a strong horizontal line by hanging artwork in an even line (as opposed to descending down the stairs) or by hanging a piece of directional art (meaning that something in the picture points up the stairs). To counteract the downward flow and draw the nourishing energy up to other parts of your home, place a seating area at the top of the stairs, or a great work of art, to lift your gaze and the energy upward. In Feng Shui, round, multi-faceted crystals (approximately the size of a ping-pong ball) mediate energy flow, so you could suspend a crystal from the ceiling at the bottom or top of the stairs. (See Resources.)

Hallways. If your nursery is located at the end of a long, empty hallway, the energy may be entering the room too quickly. To slow down the energy in a hallway, you could suspend a crystal halfway down the hall. Lighting the hallway also helps slow down the energy, as does an area rug. Anything that captures your attention and causes you to pause as you walk down the hallway—such as art, bookshelves, or plants—will also make the energy slow down.

Windows across from doors. If you enter a room or home and immediately see a window, often the energy will rush too quickly through the room and out the window without reaching the other parts of the room. To balance this situation, consider suspending a crystal from the ceiling midway between the door and window, or hanging a crystal in the window, which can give the room a wonderful rainbow light. A wind chime is another option. You could also use a piece of furniture to slow down the energy. Square and rectangular furniture will slow it down and round furniture will recirculate the energy in all the directions. Another option is to place a plant in front of the window to help contain the energy.

Bathrooms in bedrooms. Bathrooms are places where the energy (along with the water) goes down and out. Bathrooms that are in a bedroom can send too much energy out of the room, which can leave you feeling drained. If your nursery is connected to a bathroom, you should 1) keep the bathroom door closed; 2) suspend a crystal in the bathroom to circulate the energy; or 3) enhance the bathroom with upward growing plants, the color green to represent nature, or artwork that depicts upward movement like balloons, butterflies, and birds.

Beams, slanted ceilings, and eaves. Pay special attention to rooms with beams, slanted ceilings, or eaves. Eaves and slanted ceilings may force you to stoop or duck, disrupting your movement through a space. And just as your movement is disturbed, the flow of energy in a room is interrupted as well. These structures also push energy downward, creating an overhead pressure. Place any furniture or items that you use frequently out from under the slanted part of the ceiling so you rarely have to stoop. Heavy beams overhead are also a perceived danger. Although

you know the beam won't fall and hurt you, your body registers the uncomfortable feeling of something heavy hanging over your head. If you have beams in your nursery, try to position the crib between the beams. You may further correct this problem by painting the beams and eaves the same color as the ceiling. You may also place a lamp that shines upward under the beam to balance the energy pushing down.

Energy movement. Slow energy is as uncomfortable as fast energy. The best way to keep energy from stagnating in a room is to remove clutter and excess furniture. You can then arrange your furniture in a way that will help the energy circulate. Placing your furniture in Command Positions will invite energy into a room. You want to be able to walk into a room without being stopped by an object. You do not want to feel like you have to walk around things or turn your shoulder to fit by furniture. If you need to squeeze your body in some way to move through a room, the energy then has to squeeze as well. Lamps also help to lift the energy in a room, and for this reason they are particularly effective in corners where the energy tends to stagnate.

Quick Tips:

• Go through your home and look for anything that may be an actual or perceived danger. Perceived danger is anything that makes you uncomfortable because it appears dangerous. Remove or adjust anything that causes discomfort.

• Open your windows every day to allow in fresh air and help decrease indoor air pollution.

• Place a mat or basket by the front door where your family and guests can leave their shoes. A shoeless home will reduce the amount of outdoor pesticides and chemicals that are tracked in on your shoes.

• Look at how you use the rooms in your home. Could a room you rarely use serve another purpose?

• Decide if you want to make each room in your home baby-friendly or if some rooms will be off-limits. In baby-friendly rooms place fragile objects on higher shelves and consider slipcovers for the furniture.

• To help energy flow, be mindful of furniture arrangement. Track your eye movement through a room. You want your gaze to be gently drawn to different areas of the room, not to rush too quickly through the space or to get stuck on one object. Make sure you can easily move in and out of rooms without heavy furniture or clutter blocking your path. Placing your furniture in Command Position also allows the energy to move more freely.

Chapter Five

What You Will Need

Many new parents are more overwhelmed by the amount of baby stuff they are told they need than they are by the prospect of actually caring for their baby. They can be intimidated by unfamiliar products like "wipes warmers" or "bumper covers," or by the prospect of working a breast pump or installing a car seat. More and more baby gear is available, and becoming more and more stylish and technologically sophisticated, but although some of the new equipment may be very useful, much of it is not. In fact, some of the things friends and stores lead you to believe are indispensable simply end up becoming clutter that takes up space and wastes your time. It's very common to think (and wish) that some new piece of baby equipment will make parenting easy, but that's never been the case, nor will it ever be. Keep in mind that what you could buy and what you actually need are two different things.

When it comes down to it, the only things you *really* need in the first few months are: diapers, wipes, blankets, some onesies that snap, and milk. At the same time, if you have always dreamed of creating a lavish nursery, then by all means indulge your fantasies and don't feel pressured to create too streamlined or minimalist a nursery. If you've always waited for the moment when you could pick out expensive, beautiful baby clothes, then don't let an experienced mom who knows the hassle of hard-to-put-on outfits (that your baby quickly outgrows) talk you out of it. Just be aware that it's a choice, not a necessity.

Preparation and Organization

Most parents will agree that a prepared and organized environment is helpful. You have enough to learn about caring for your child in the first few weeks without running to stores to purchase things or learning how to use new equipment. The key is to find the balance between too much stuff, and what will help make taking care of your baby easier. Trying to figure out what will work for you before you've experienced being a parent makes it all the more challenging (for instance, it's difficult to know whether you would prefer a nursing pillow or not if you have never nursed before). You will have your own unique style and preferences, but it may be helpful to spend time around other new parents to get a feel for what they think is useful. Visit their nurseries and see what makes sense to you. Ask friends whose parenting style you admire what they find useful.

It's a good idea to have your nursery set up one month in advance of your due date. This way if your baby comes early you're prepared, and if not, you have the last month of pregnancy to rest up for labor and birth. It takes longer than you might expect to set things up; even when you have everything purchased and in the room, you still need to unpack, clean, and organize it all. In addition, you'll want to learn how to use equipment, such as bottle sterilizers, strollers, or any other gadgets that require instructions. After your baby is born, it will be difficult to focus and find time to read instructions.

You will also want to install your car seat well in advance. Hospitals will not discharge your baby if you don't have a properly installed car seat, and they're not allowed to help you install it. For help installing your car seat, you can visit an inspection station or contact a Child Passenger Safety Technician. (For more information about car seat safety visit the National Highway Traffic Safety Administration [NHTSA] website, nhtsa.gov.) Don't let your first challenge as a new parent be the unnecessary stress of trying to install the car seat as your partner and baby wait to go home.

Where you have it is as important as what you have, so make sure that everything is easily accessible. Caring for a baby involves many repetitive rituals and the ease with which you perform them will contribute to your sense of well-being. For example, changing a diaper eight times a day is less stressful if you have a comfortable changing table with diapers, wipes, and clothes easily accessible and organized.

The Nursing Area

The most important things you'll want to have in the nursing area are a comfy chair that supports your back and a place to rest your feet. You will be spending a great deal of time in that chair holding, feeding, and soothing your infant, so make sure it's as comfortable as possible. If you want your nursing chair to glide or rock, you can choose a traditional rocking chair and rest your feet on a stool, or a glider that comes with padding and a gliding footrest. You could also choose an upholstered chair and ottoman that glides.

You may want a side table next to the chair. Once you sit down to nurse, it can be frustrating not to have everything you need within reach. Many nursing mothers find it helpful to time feedings. Position a glow-in-the-dark clock so you can see it from the nursing chair. Locate the clock at least six feet away or choose a battery-operated clock to reduce the EMFs. A dim lamp is also helpful, but again due to EMFs, you may wish to place the lamp six feet away from you and your baby. You may also need space on your table for bottles, a bottle warmer, a burp cloth, and possibly a breast pump. Be aware

The comfortable chair and round side table make this nursing area both practical and inviting.

that certain kinds of plastic (such as PVC and polycarbonate) used to make some baby bottles can, when heated, leach potentially harmful chemicals into the milk. Glass baby bottles are a good alternative to plastic. For freezing milk, look for milk storage bags or bottles that are made of polyethylene or polypropylene plastic, which has not been known to leach harmful chemicals. (For more information about plastic bottles visit The Green Guide website, thegreenguide.com.)

Nursing mothers may want to buy comfortable all-cotton nursing bras as well as a nursing nightgown and a warm robe.

Things to consider for the nursing area:

- *Nursing chair*
- *Burp cloths (cloth diapers make excellent burp cloths)*
- *Clock*
- *Lamp*
- *Bottles: Four 4 oz. bottles for the beginning and four 8 oz. bottles for later*
- *Breast pump*
- *Plastic bottles or bags for storing milk in the freezer*
- *Bottle warmer (for night feedings, it can be helpful to have a bottle warmer so you don't need to go to the kitchen to prepare bottles)*

Nursing items you will keep in the kitchen:

- *Bottle brush for cleaning bottles*
- *Bottle sterilizer (you can also use the dishwasher to sterilize bottles though you may want a dishwasher-safe basket to hold the nipples)*

The Changing Area

You will want to make sure you have a suitable and appropriately configured place to change your baby. You can buy a changing table or convert a dresser into a changing table by buying a padded cushion made for just this purpose. A changing table that is the proper height will support your back during the next two to three years of diaper changing. Since you will never want to leave your baby unattended on the changing table, simple things like having diapers and wipes close at hand are important. For this reason, you may want to have easily accessible drawers so that you can pull out items while keeping one hand on your baby.

You will also want to make a decision about using cloth or disposable diapers. There are a number of issues to consider when making this choice: the effect on the environment, the use of synthetic chemicals, cost, and convenience.

Disposable diapers leave nonbiodegradable plastics in landfills, but cloth diapers can also harm the environment due to pesticides used to treat the cotton. Cloth diapers made from organically grown, unbleached, untreated cotton may be the best choice for the environment. As for the overall cost, cloth diapers, which can be used again and again, will probably be less expensive than disposable diapers. However, disposable diapers may be much more convenient. If you plan to use disposable diapers, look for those that are gel-, latex-, perfume-, and dye-free, or made without chlorine bleaching which is better for the environment and contains fewer chemicals. (See Resources.)

For the first three months, it is best to use 100 percent cotton cloth wipes. Some companies offer organically grown, unbleached cotton wipes. If you do eventually switch to disposable wipes, the healthiest choice are those that are alcohol-, perfume-, and dye-free. (For more information, visit the Children's Health Environmental Coalition website, checnet.org.)

You may also want to have a lap pad to place on the center of the changing table so if you have a leaky diaper you don't have to change the entire table cover. For the same reason, you might also consider putting a burp cloth under your baby's head in case he spits up. An important addition to the changing area is the diaper pail. Look for a diaper pail that is specifically made for diaper disposal, since a regular trashcan probably won't seal tightly enough to keep unpleasant odors in. Alternatively, you can choose to use a small basket, but expect to empty it frequently.

The changing area can also be a play area for a newborn as well as a place for infant massage and air baths. You will be changing your baby many times a day, so you may want to give your baby a nice view with a mobile or artwork. Talk to your baby as you go about changing, dressing, and grooming, explaining each step along the way.

The changing table often becomes a play area for a newborn,
so you may wish to keep toys nearby.

Things to consider for the changing area:

- *Changing table*
- *Pad for changing table with cover*
- *Lap pad*
- *Diaper pail*
- *Laundry hamper*
- *Cloth or disposable diapers*
- *Cloth wipes*
- *Plastic bin for soiled cloth wipes*
- *Wipes warmer (Warms cloth and disposable wipes. Also keeps cloth wipes moist, so you don't need to carry your baby to the bathroom to wet them.)*
- *Natural diaper cream*
- *Grooming kit (comb, brush, nail clippers, and file)*
- *Almond oil for massage*
- *Mobile*

The Bathing Area

Bath time can be a great deal of fun for you and your baby. Babies are very slippery when wet, so it can often be more relaxing for both of you to bathe her in a sink lined with a towel, or in a baby bathtub that has a built-in support system. Babies love to play in water by kicking their feet; when they're older, they like to play with bath toys.

Since you will never leave your baby unattended in the bathtub, plan to have everything you need readily accessible. You may want to buy a wire basket to hold bath toys, or a set of drawers that you can place near the tub for

*The happy yellow ducks
and bath toys make
bathing fun.*

all your grooming supplies. Be conscious of what products you choose to use on your baby. Until your baby becomes more active and is crawling around, you probably only need to wash with water. When you do use products, choose organic or natural shampoos and body washes rather than soaps that contain harsh chemicals.

Things to consider for the bath area:

- *Baby bathtub*
- *Soft towels and washcloth*
- *Organic or natural shampoo and body wash (for when your baby gets older—water is sufficient for a newborn)*
- *Almond or olive oil for cradle cap*
- *Brush*
- *Bath toys*

The Sleeping Area

For the first few months you may choose to have your baby sleep in your room. Some parents bring the baby into their bed and others place the baby in a bassinet or cradle nearby or in a co-sleeper, which is like a small crib that attaches to the parents' bed. A cradle is a great option because you can see and rock your baby without having to get out of bed. At some point, you may wish to transition your baby from your room to the nursery, or from a cradle to a crib. When looking for a crib, safety should be at the forefront of your mind. Look for a certification seal that indicates the crib has met federal safety standards. Make sure the crib slats are no more than 2⅜ inches apart and that crib posts are not over ¹⁄₁₆ of an inch high. (For more information about crib safety, visit the Juvenile Products Manufacturers Association website, jpma.org, or the National Safety Council website, nsc.org.) If you choose a metal crib, be sure it doesn't have any sharp angles that could be dangerous. Check to make sure that the side of the crib is easy to maneuver up and down and moves quietly.

Pay very close attention to what you put in the crib. A baby spends almost half of the day asleep with her nose and mouth only inches away from the mattress and bedding, so make sure that the crib is as toxin-free an environment as possible. Mattresses made of synthetic materials, and the flame retardants used to treat them, can contain a host of chemicals that emit toxic fumes. All-natural, untreated wool mattresses are an excellent, healthy alternative. In addition to being chemical-free, untreated wool helps maintain a comfortable body temperature; wicks away moisture; resists mold, mildew, and dust mites; and is naturally flame-resistant. If you do purchase a mattress made from synthetic materials, place your mattress outside for at least a month so some of the chemicals will off-gas before placing it in the nursery. Wool puddle pads are an excellent alternative to plastic under-sheets. (See Resources.) Also, be sure to buy a firm mattress that fits tightly into the crib; a firm mattress reduces the risk of suffocation and a snug fitting mattress eliminates any chance of your baby getting stuck between the crib and mattress.

You will also need a fitted sheet. For healthier bedding look for 100 percent cotton sheets that do not say "wrinkle free" or "permanent press," which indicates they have probably been treated with chemicals. You could also buy sheets and blankets made from organically grown cotton that comes with a guarantee that it has never been treated with pesticides. (See Resources.) Always wash sheets before their first use. Use an unscented, chemical-free laundry detergent. To prevent suffocation, do not put any pillows, plush blankets, or toys in the crib. If you want to use a bumper, make sure it is securely tied to the crib slats and not too plush. While bumpers can keep your baby from bumping her head or getting a foot or hand stuck in the crib slats, a bumper could be a suffocation hazard, and as your baby learns to stand, the bumper may give her added height so she can climb (and fall) out of the crib—you may wish to skip the bumper altogether.

A great option for your baby's daytime naps is a Moses basket (a wicker basket with mattress and liner), which is easily carried from room to room. Although Moses baskets are not recommended for nighttime sleeping (they usually have too much padding around a newborn's face), they are excellent for keeping an eye on your baby while taking care of other things, such as taking a shower, paying bills, or cooking a meal. If your home has two levels and you're considering buying a portable crib for travel, it can double as an excellent downstairs bed or play area. Many portable cribs come with a bassinet feature where your baby can lie or sit higher up and interact with you.

Things to consider for the sleeping area:

- *Crib*
- *Crib mattress*
- *Crib sheet (at least two)*
- *Crib skirt (similar to a bed skirt)*
- *Wool puddle pad*
- *Receiving blankets for swaddling (at least two)*

- *Moses basket*
- *Bassinet, cradle, or co-sleeper*
- *Mattress, sheets, and wool puddle pad for your bassinet or co-sleeper*
- *Baby monitors (place at least six feet away from the crib)*

The Play Area

It is very easy to stimulate a newborn. Just think about all the things that your baby is taking in simply by eating, being changed, and interacting with your home. Getting dressed, taking a bath, exploring a new room and home, and getting to know you is a lot of stimulation. Talking, singing, and dancing with your baby is also great entertainment. Taking your baby on a "tour of your house," and speaking slowly and rhythmically about everything in your home, is a great "game." Often the best entertainment is found in nature, going for walks outside, or placing your baby on his back so he can see the trees dance in the wind or watch the birds fly. You can also take a simple object, like a colorful scarf, and gently wave it in front of your baby. Babies also like to look at themselves, so a mirror placed in front of them can be a great activity. Newborns really don't need toys. Simply giving your baby different "views of the world" is great stimulation.

Similarly, even older children don't need complicated, bright, multi-colored, loud toys. Keep the toys simple and few; opt for wooden toys instead of bringing more plastics into your home. Many children's toys, particularly (and ironically) teethers, are made with PVC and toxic softeners known as phthalates. When children put toys containing PVCs in their mouths, the toxic additives leak out. Remember that just about everything will probably end up in your baby's mouth. Most likely you will have some plastic toys, such as toys for the bath, so keep in mind it is better for your child's health to avoid plastics made

A comfortable place to play on the floor and a few toys
are all you need to create a play area.

with PVCs. (To find out which toy manufacturers are still using PVCs and which have eliminated PVCs, visit the Greenpeace website, greenpeaceusa.org.)

Children also need quiet time and empty space. If you want them to cultivate a sense of inner peace then you will want to create that in their environment by creating quiet, empty space. The faster and louder toys and video games become, the more children look for that kind of external stimulation instead of developing the imagination and inner resources to entertain themselves. Also, no matter how many toys you have, or what kind, the chances are that mundane things such as phones and spoons will always get the most attention. Many people have experienced giving a child a gift only to find she is much more interested in the box the gift came in than the gift itself.

A mat or blanket for the floor or a natural fiber area rug is probably the most important thing you will need for a play area. Your baby will need to have some stomach time each day, so find a comfortable, natural fiber rug, mat, or blanket for her to lie on. As she gets older, the rug will be a good, comfortable place to learn how to crawl. If you do not have wood or cork floors or natural fiber carpeting, it is especially important to create a barrier between your carpeting and your baby via a natural fiber play mat. (See Resources.)

Children are accustomed to movement in the womb, and for this reason swings and bouncy seats can be soothing; however, some doctors believe it can strain your baby's back to be placed in a sitting position before he is ready, so you may want to keep the seats fully reclined until your baby has the strength to sit up on his own. You can avoid investing in plastic ExerSaucers or other items that contain your child by creating a gated-off "safe" zone. This way your child can play and you can get things done without having to force him to stand or sit up before he is ready. As your child gets older, you may want to get a low table and small chairs for eating, reading, or drawing.

Another consideration for the play area is storage. You will want furniture with easy-access storage such as bookshelves with cabinet doors, bins, baskets, or a toy chest.

Things to consider for the play area:

- *Toy storage such as bookcases, cabinets, toy boxes, bins, or baskets*
- *Floor mat*
- *Mobile*
- *Colorful scarf*
- *Books*
- *Music (CD player and CDs)*
- *Rattles*
- *Wood teethers*
- *Mirror*

Clothes

When you're selecting clothes, it is best to focus on comfortable, everyday, durable basics that are easy to get on and off. Onesies that snap all the way down are great because they are comfortable for sleeping but they also work as day clothes for outings, playing, and visitors. Most likely you will receive special outfits as gifts from friends and family.

Buy 100 percent cotton clothes and wash everything in advance with an all-natural detergent. Avoid clothes that have been treated with chemicals such as stain repellants or that say "wrinkle-free" or "permanent press." It is also a good idea to remove any scratchy tags. You may want to hang the clothes for later months in the closet by size so you don't forget about them; often clothes received as gifts and stored for later use are discovered in a drawer long after the baby has outgrown them.

Clothes to consider:

- *Gowns that snap in the front and have a drawstring bottom*
- *Long- and short-sleeve snap or side-tie tees*
- *Pull-on elastic pants and snap shirts*
- *Onesies*
- *Sweaters*
- *Socks*
- *Moccasin socks*
- *Booties*
- *Bibs*
- *Cotton mittens*
- *Caps*
- *Coat (for cold weather climates)*

Other Things to Consider

Packing for the hospital. Honor your personality. If you're more comfortable with lots of things from home, then bring whatever will make you feel good. If you feel overwhelmed by stuff and suitcases, just bring the necessities. Either way, remember that this is the room where you will labor and your child will be born. A simple way to create a sacred space for delivery is to take time during the month before your baby is born to imagine the hospital room filled with a white, healing light and ask that the room be cleared of any stagnant energy and filled with loving energy. You may also choose to enhance the energy in the room with some of your treasured objects. For instance, bring a photograph of you and your partner or some music, which will help lift the vibration in the room.

You may also want to create a list of phone numbers of people you will want to call once your baby is born. You may call some people yourself and ask a friend or family member to call others for you. Finally, pack an outfit for going home. Select loose-fitting clothing; you will likely have a belly the same size as you did between your fourth and sixth months of pregnancy. For your baby, you will want a coming home outfit that includes a onesie, a cap, a receiving blanket, and possibly mittens, booties, and an extra blanket depending on your climate. The hospital will send you home with diapers and supplies that should take care of your needs if you have a long drive home.

Buy a first aid kit. You will want to have a basic first aid kit in your home, as well as a nasal aspirator. It is also a good idea to take an infant safety and CPR class prior to the birth of your baby.

Register for gifts. One bonus to registering is that a salesperson will take you around and guide you, telling you what you may want and how things work. Also, registering helps you prevent accumulating clutter because you can let people know what it is you really need and like. Buy thank-you cards and stamps before you give birth, so that when gifts start coming in you're ready to send a thank-you note. But don't worry about being timely with your notes—everyone understands that you've just had a baby.

Outings. You may wish to have a baby bag—either a true baby bag or a bag you convert—that goes wherever the baby goes, carrying diapers, wipes, a changing pad, an extra set of clothes, burp clothes, bottles if you are bottle feeding, and a blanket. Get in the habit of restocking the bag after every outing so you always have a baby bag packed and ready to go. You will also want some infant carriers, which allow you to carry the baby and still be hands free. Consider a BabyBjörn or a sling. You will also want a stroller and stroller blankets. You can get one that will hold your infant car seat so that if your baby falls asleep while you're driving, you don't have to wake her up to bring her with you.

Plan storage now. Children grow and change so quickly that their no-longer-used items or outgrown clothes can take over the room, making finding things difficult. Think ahead. It's so easy to get behind, and overwhelmed, and the

Hanging clothes by size even if they are too big now, will remind you of what you already own as your baby grows.

more you do now the better. Leave drawers and shelves and closet space empty and buy storage containers. Decide now if you plan on keeping outgrown clothes and toys. Get the bins or find the place where you will store the items you decide to keep.

Plan birth announcements. Prepare a list of addresses for people you will want to send a birth announcement to. If you choose your birth announcement in advance, designate a friend or family member to be in charge of phoning in the birth information, such as time, place, weight, and height.

Organize photographs. It's so enjoyable to page through baby albums, but it's easy to get overwhelmed by stacks of photos and never catch up. Get a system in place before your baby is born. Take twelve photo boxes or twelve large envelopes and label them Month One, Month Two, etc., for the first twelve months. At the very least, your photos will be sorted in chronological order right away, even if you don't have time to place them in albums. Children love looking at pictures of themselves and hearing about his or her life as a "little baby." Consider a few nonbreakable picture frames or cloth photo albums for your baby to enjoy and touch.

Purchase a convertible sofa bed or twin bed. If you have enough space in the nursery, you may want a place to sleep on those nights when you are feeding a lot, or if you just want to give your partner a break from waking up with you every few hours. The advantage of a twin bed is that your baby will eventually grow into it.

Travel

In order to make traveling with a baby as graceful as possible, it helps to plan early and be prepared. It takes more time than you might think to organize your baby's necessities for a trip, so you might want to begin packing a week in advance. Determining what to bring depends, of course, on where you're going, how long you'll be away, and also on your personality. If you like to have all your specific brands with you and don't want to worry about needing more supplies, then pack everything from a bottle brush to formula to laundry detergent. If you don't mind taking some time from your trip or vacation to shop and know that you can find what you need, then you can carry less with you. Just make sure you have enough of the essentials such as formula and diapers to get you through the first few days in case what you need is not readily available. Since babies' clothes are so small, it may be more enjoyable to just pack more, or depending on the situation, it might be easier to run a few loads of laundry. If you're staying at a hotel call in advance to see if they offer any supplies. Some hotels have cribs, changing tables, high chairs, diaper pails, and will even cover the electrical outlets in your room. It's a good idea to bring a few of your own blankets, however, as babies are more easily soothed and sleep better in a new place if they're surrounded by things that smell like home. You will also want to bring with you anything that may be essential to helping your baby sleep, such as a particular book or blanket. As your child gets older, you won't want her to be accustomed to bringing lots of toys and stuffed animals on trips. Too many belongings can get overwhelming, but if your baby is attached to one blanket or animal that is an important part of the bedtime routine, bring it with you. If you're flying, don't take the risk of checking it—carry it on the plane. You can use it to help your baby understand that the best thing to do on an airplane is sleep. If you are very lucky and your baby sleeps the whole time, take some time to rest yourself.

As important as what items you bring is the bag you carry them in. It can be frustrating, particularly if your baby is on your lap, to have to rummage through a big bag searching for something. Find a baby bag with many different compartments. Choose one secure and accessible compartment for keeping important items such as your wallet and tickets. You can also pack a few small items in large, clear plastic bags so you can easily see things. And always pack anything that can leak in plastic! If you're traveling alone, you may want to consider using a backpack for carry-on items, and a sling or some other type of carrier for your baby. You can also bring your stroller and check it right before you board the plane. If you pay for a seat for your baby, it's safer and easier to bring your car seat on the plane.

Include enough diapers and wipes so that you'll be prepared in the event of any delays. Bring plastic bags to dispose of dirty diapers and a changing pad (many baby bags come equipped with a changing pad, otherwise you can buy one separately). Also pack a few changes of clothes and a blanket or an extra sweater to keep your baby warm on the plane. If you are traveling from a warm climate to a cold climate or vice versa make sure you have an appropriate outfit to put on your baby right before you land or as soon as you get off the plane. You may also want an additional blanket to place over the seat and armrest so that your baby does not get her hands and mouth all over them. It is usually easier to pack a few bottles so you don't have to worry about trying to clean or sterilize a bottle on the plane. If you nurse or give your baby a bottle on the ascent and descent it will help keep her ears clear. You may want to have something for your baby to put in her mouth if she is teething. Also carry with you any medications or pain relievers. As your baby gets older, you will want to pack a meal, snacks, and as much "entertainment" as you can, such as crayons, DVDs, books, and maybe even a few surprises.

If you're traveling by car you will want to have a bag that you keep in the front that has the same essentials that are mentioned above. This way, you do not have to rummage through a tightly packed trunk to find an extra change of clothes, etc. If you don't have tinted windows in your car, consider a car shade to keep the sun out which will help your baby sleep. Also include your baby's favorite music. For older children, it's a good idea to pack a cooler with drinks, plenty of water, snacks, and meals.

Traveling with young children can be challenging. In addition to organizing your belongings, take some time to prepare mentally and energetically. Set an intention that your trip flow smoothly, that you experience optimal health, and get to where you are going with the utmost ease on time and in time. You may even write down a series of affirmations describing an ideal trip. Also take time to communicate with your baby. Explain where you are going, what will happen, and what is to be expected.

Quick Tips

• Take the time to learn how to use all your baby equipment before your baby is born.

• Spend time at a friend's house seeing what things you really think will be helpful and what you can do without. Do you have friends or relatives who might be willing to loan you strollers, bassinets, cribs, etc.?

• Have the car seat installed and nursery ready at least one month in advance of your due date.

• Wash all baby clothes, blankets, and bed linens in an all-natural detergent one month in advance of your due date.

• Decide if you will keep baby equipment and outgrown clothes and toys. If so, plan your storage system before your baby is born. Buy storage containers and make room in closets, drawers, or other parts of your home.

• Consider registering for gifts. Your friends' and families' money and time will be well spent and you will have the added benefit of a salesperson who can help familiarize you with the baby equipment.

Chapter Six

Enhancing the Nursery

Now that you have a clean, fresh room filled with the necessities, it's time to add the magic. Fill the room with warmth and love by adding meaningful objects and art, beautiful reminders of nature, and fabrics and texture that nurture the senses. Your nursery can be an enchanted place filled with objects and decorations that stimulate, engage, and comfort your baby. As you prepare the room, your parenting has already begun. Decorating the nursery offers an opportunity to express your greatest wishes for your baby by creating joyful surroundings.

Decorating from the Heart

Decorating from the heart means designing a space from the inside out. Interior design often focuses on the externals—how something *looks* rather than how it makes you *feel*. While aesthetics are important, equally important is how a room makes you feel. Before running out to the stores, take a moment to visualize the nursery you hope to create. Try not to be influenced by what you think a nursery "should" look like; instead, take a moment to get in touch with how you want it to feel. Make a list of several feelings you would like the nursery to evoke, such as tranquility and love.

Especially during the first few months, the nursery is as much for you as it is for your baby. You'll be spending a lot of time in the nursery, so you should feel

Simply removing packaging makes even a stack of diapers look attractive.

a sense of peace and joy when you're in the room. Since your baby can't tell you how he or she would like the nursery to look, decorate in a way that sparks your own sense of wonder and imagination. Your unique expression is what will make this room so special.

If you have the time, and enjoy decorating, create an inspiration board for the nursery. Get a large piece of thick paper and tape on paint samples, fabric swatches, or photos from magazines and catalogs that you like. This will give you a pretty good idea of the feel of the room you're creating and help you avoid spending hours shopping aimlessly. At the top of the board, write down the list you wrote of feelings you want the nursery to evoke.

Keep in mind that every corner of the space does not need to be filled; empty space is okay and can even encourage peace and quiet. Just as you would not fill a child's schedule with activities from morning to night, you do not need to fill his space with objects from wall to wall. In Feng Shui, the center of the room is often left open to help the energy circulate more freely.

As a parent you will give so much of your energy to your child that you will want to be inspired by your surroundings. You don't need to spend a lot of money to create a beautiful room. It is often the simple, inexpensive things with special meaning, or careful placement that really speak to you. Even diapers, removed from their packaging and placed in a wicker basket, can be beautiful. When selecting decorative elements take into account health, meaning, and function—choose things that not only improve the look of your nursery, but also support your physical, emotional, mental, and spiritual well-being.

Enhancements

The decorations you place in the nursery should not only be beautiful, but should enhance your life by being inspirational and meaningful, which is why you can think of decorations as not just pretty objects, but as enhancements. When decorated properly, your home becomes a positive affirmation that lifts your energy, boosts your self-esteem, and reinforces your goals. Every object that is consciously placed in the nursery will create positive energy and enhance your experience and your baby's experience in that room.

Keep in mind, even objects we may consider inanimate have a life force. How you respond to their vibrations as well as how you feel about these objects can affect you either positively or negatively. Imagine a shell from a beach next to a pinecone from a forest. Even though the pinecone and the shell may both be inanimate objects of approximately the same size, each has its own unique vibration. When we look at a shell it reminds us of the ocean and connects us to the powerful energy of the ocean. The pinecone's energy is the quieter, more peaceful energy of a forest.

Now imagine that you found the shell on a beach while taking a walk with your spouse on your honeymoon, and that you found the pinecone minutes after receiving bad news. You now have personal associations with the shell and the pinecone that intensify their vibration because of the memories and feelings that each evokes. Your own energy is affected—either positively or negatively—by the objects that surround you. When you select enhancements for the nursery, surround yourself and your baby with things that have a positive vibration and personal association, both of which will boost your energy and lift your spirits.

You may also choose objects that support your goals. For example, if you want to improve your relationship with your family, you may want to place a family photo from a particularly happy time in the kitchen where you and your family can see it often and be reminded of that feeling of happiness you shared. Or if you want to nurture your child's creative expression, you could display artwork in the nursery. Each time you see the enhancement, you place your attention on your goal. Enhancements are anything you choose to place in your home to either support your goals or make you feel good about yourself and others.

Nursery Enhancements

Children, who are just developing a sense of self, need positive affirmations more than anyone. Your child's interactions with his room will be his first interactions with the world. He learns how the world works by exploring and playing with his environment. Create a room that is filled with enhancements that make your child feel loved and supported, and that boost self-esteem. A room filled with positive enhancements will help your child develop a positive view of himself and the world.

Meaningful objects and things you love. Anything that has positive, personal significance to you is an enhancement. Your association with the object will trigger a memory and a feeling that creates a unique energy. If the object is a good enhancement, then the memory is a happy one, and the feeling the item

Colorful toys and happy animals are wonderful nursery enhancements.

evokes is positive. For instance, gifts from friends and family carry the energy of those people, so by placing those items around the nursery you are surrounding yourself and your baby with the support and love of all those people. However, if you receive a gift from someone that you don't currently have a good relationship with, such as a coworker you frequently quibble with or an estranged family member, then when you see the gift you will be reminded of that unfortunate relationship, and your energy will be drained instead of uplifted. So check and make sure each object you place in the nursery has a positive association.

Photographs. Photographs trigger memories of the people and events in the photo. When the people in the photos are your loved ones and the memories are happy, photographs are powerful, positive enhancements. A family photograph of you and your partner cradling your newborn is an excellent enhancement for the nursery. When you view the photograph you will be reminded not only of the miracle of life, but of your partner's support. The photo will also help your baby feel loved and secure.

Photographs of your baby with his siblings during a happy, loving moment are a wonderful way to encourage positive relationships among your children. If your children share a room, place a photograph of them during a happy time in a place where they can both see it every day. If they are in separate rooms, place a photo in each room. Photographs of loving grandparents who may live far away are also an excellent way to bring the grandparents' energy into the nursery. Photos of grandparents and very close family friends remind both you and the baby that you have a large support system that extends beyond that room. However, do not overload the nursery with photographs, as images of people usually have a very active energy that is not always conducive to sleep. Some photos may be better placed in family rooms or kitchens where your family spends a lot of time awake.

Artwork. Artwork is a great enhancement. You may find a piece of art in which the image is meaningful to you, or you may simply find the colors of a particular artwork uplifting. Either way, the artwork will enhance your nursery. Be creative when looking for nursery art. If you have a favorite children's story, consider framing illustrations from the book. You can frame pretty wrapping paper or gift cards. You can also try to make your own artwork. Take out paper, pens, crayons, stamps, ink, stencils, or paint and be creative. If you have older children, include them in the decorating process by asking them if they would like to create an artwork for the baby's room. Objects that are handmade by an artist carry a different energy than objects that are manufactured by machine; objects made by your own hand carry your own unique, loving energy.

Nature. Bring the power of nature to the nursery with plants or artwork depicting trees, animals, rivers, or any scene from nature. You can also bring in natural objects such as large seashells and fresh flowers. (Make sure the shells are large enough that they're not a choking hazard.) Furniture and objects made from wood, or fabrics made from natural linen, hemp, or raffia also connect you to nature. Consider bringing nature to your window by placing a bird feeder in a nearby tree. Imagine your baby's delight as she watches birds fly around outside the window. Enhancing your nursery with reminders of nature or natural materials is especially important if you live in an urban environment where it's easy to feel disconnected from nature.

Color. As discussed throughout this book, color is a powerful enhancement because it can affect your mood (see page 41). Paint color looks very different on a wall than it does on a sample chip, so test it by painting a large area, such as half a wall. Light will also significantly change the appearance, so check to see how the color looks at different times of day, as well as at night.

Things that stimulate the senses. Anything that stimulates the senses in a positive way will produce good energy. Your baby will be learning about the world through her exploration of her room, so try to engage all of your baby's senses: smell, sight, touch, taste, and sound. Contrast different textures such as plush stuffed animals and smooth hardwood floors for your baby to stimulate her sense of touch. Stimulate her sense of smell (and help protect yours) by placing fragrant flowers near the changing table or opening a window to let in the smell of the outdoors. Use different colors and patterns to stimulate her eyesight. Hang wind chimes or sing lullabies to create beautiful sounds. And stimulate her taste buds by simply providing milk!

Written affirmations. Writing a positive affirmation is a wonderful way to set an intention for your life and your baby's life. For example, you may set an intention for your child to always be surrounded by loving and supportive people. You would then write, using the present tense, "I am surrounded by love." Place the piece of paper underneath an object in the room or in a box. You may also choose to make the affirmation visible by framing the piece of paper or writing it on the wall. Some people like to write nursery rhymes on the wall; however, many classic nursery rhymes tell surprisingly unsettling stories, so think twice about the message you're sending your child. Create or find quotes that will support your baby and send a positive message.

View. A pleasing view naturally enhances a room. A view from a window is representative of how you feel about the outside world. You'll want your child to have a positive view of the world. If the view outside the window is less than ideal, consider hanging scrim curtain panels that will allow in sunlight, but block the unappealing view. You could also purchase bottom up shades that allow sunlight to enter unobstructed from the top of the window, but block an undesirable view from eye level. Another option could be to install a window box filled with plants and flowers. Make sure windows are safely protected by guards.

Also check your child's view from the crib. What you see when you start your day and what you see at the end of your day has a powerful effect on your state of mind. An example of a less-than-ideal view would be a toilet, which Feng Shui believes can be a drain on your health. If the toilet is in view from the crib, keep the bathroom door closed, enhance the bathroom, and consider suspending a crystal just inside the bathroom door midway between the door and toilet. Conversely, a great view from the crib would be a beautiful work of art.

Energy Enhancements

Enhancements are also anything that lifts and circulates the energy in your home. Even if your home is filled with positive affirmations, if energy is not uplifted and circulating freely throughout it you will be less able to appreciate and enjoy your affirmations. Imagine a painting used to inspire creativity hanging in a dark corner, or a happy family photo on a cluttered counter. Each object's positive impact is affected by its surroundings. Now imagine the painting in a brightly lit corner or the family photo on an organized, clean counter: the impact is much stronger.

Light. Lighting can set the mood in a room. For instance, dim lights will probably make you feel relaxed and sleepy, while bright lights might make you feel more awake and active. Lighting is a very effective way to change the energy in a room. Add bright lights or open curtains to let in sunlight any time you want to energize a space. Place lamps in dark corners or areas where the energy seems stagnant to help the energy circulate and flow throughout every nook and cranny of a room.

Mirrors. Mirrors increase the energy in a room by reflecting and therefore doubling positive images. If a plant is placed in front of a mirror the benefits of the plant will be doubled; if it reflects beautiful artwork then the meaning of the artwork and energy of the artwork will be doubled. Mirrors are excellent enhancements for very small rooms because they double the size of the room. A mirror in a room with few windows can be positioned so that it reflects the outdoors, doubling your view and acting as an additional window. All reflective surfaces bring more light into a room, brightening the feeling and increasing energy. Therefore they are excellent to use in a space that feels stagnant and needs to be more active, such as a room with little circulation. However, because mirrors energize a space, they can make sleep difficult, so it is not advisable to place one where you can see it while lying in bed. Also, avoid selecting a mirror that is warped and distorts your image or one that is divided into sections that will fragment images. Seeing yourself or your loved ones "in pieces" is an example of a perceived danger that causes stress. People tend to believe whatever is reflected back to them, so make sure a positive image is being reflected back to you. Finally, hang the mirror at an appropriate height so that whoever uses it can see their entire head without stooping or reaching.

Wind chimes. Wind chimes capture the energy of the wind to create sound. Sound creates a vibration that creates and attracts even more energy, making wind chimes an excellent way to attract, increase, and circulate the energy in any space.

Mobiles. The motion and color of mobiles circulate and attract energy. Mobiles that play music have the added benefit of sound, which also attracts energy.

Fountains or images of water. Moving water, such as a fountain, is particularly good for attracting and then circulating energy in a room. Even pictures of water or the sound of water can be an enhancement.

Plants. Plants create harmony in your environment by uplifting and circulating the energy. A healthy plant is a beautiful reminder of nature and enhances any area of your home. In addition to being beautiful and attracting energy, plants are believed to clean the air you breathe. Make sure that any plants placed in the nursery dry out thoroughly between waterings to avoid mold growth.

Multi-faceted round crystals. In Feng Shui crystals are believed to regulate energy by slowing energy down in a room where the energy is rushing through, and speeding energy up in a room where the energy is stagnant. They also lift energy in a room where energy rushes downward; for example in a bathroom, where the motion of water running down drains and toilets pushes the energy down and out. Crystals placed in a corner or stagnant area will circulate the energy. If placed near a window, they will catch the light and create beautiful rainbow prisms. Crystals are therefore an excellent enhancement wherever energy needs to be improved.

Creative enhancements. You can also create your own energy enhancements. For instance, if energy needs to be lifted in a bathroom use decorative shower curtain hooks that are shaped like butterflies or bees that are flying upward. The upward movement of the decorative creatures will lift the energy. You could lift the energy in a dark corner with a toy hot air balloon or rocket or you could direct energy with a model ship sailing in the direction you want the energy to flow.

A toy hot air balloon lifts the energy in this corner.

Imitating Nature

Not everyone has an "eye" for decorating so if you feel intimidated by the process of matching fabrics and paint swatches, then look to nature for inspiration. Everything in nature "matches." You would never look at a forest and think that a maple tree clashes with an oak tree or green plants and red flowers don't match the blue sky. Different types of wood don't clash—just remember the forest—so consider leaving wood furniture unpainted or leaving wooden floors bare. Adding an organic cotton throw to your nursing chair or using linen curtains will also bring in nature. By decorating with natural materials and colors that mimic elements in nature, you'll find decorating is easy.

Feng Shui uses the five elements present in nature—water, wood, fire, earth, and metal—to create peace in our homes. In Feng Shui it is believed that people are most comfortable when all of the elements are present in their surroundings. When all five elements are present in a room, a harmonious and soothing energy is created. Obviously, this doesn't mean that we must have the actual elements, such as fire, in the nursery; the elements take many forms and are represented by specific colors, shapes, and objects. For example, fire may be represented in a room by the color red, by sunlight, by images of the sun, or by triangular shapes. (See Sidebar to understand the different manifestations of the elements.)

Elements

Water: black, dark blue, mirrors, fountains, images of water, curves, meandering and flowing lines

Wood: green, sky blue, wood, plants, flowers, trees, floral patterns, fabric, images of trees, columns, pillars

Fire: red, orange, candles, sunlight, lamps, images of animals and people, animal prints, images of the sun or fire, triangles

Earth: yellow, beige, brown, ceramics, tile, terra-cotta, brick, squares, rectangles

Metal: white, pastels, metal, stones, arches, circles

Set an intention for harmony in the nursery by decorating it with a variety of colors, textures, and materials. Experimenting with the elements can be fun. Since each element is represented by a color, a simple way to balance the elements is to make sure you have a variety of colors in your nursery.

Balance

In interior design magazines you may see a lot of spaces designed in extreme ways—vast, spare spaces designed on a public, not private, scale. Often these rooms are beautiful to behold but don't look as though they'd feel good to live in. A white room may feel cold and unwelcoming, and it may be nerve-wracking to sit and eat on white furniture for fear of staining something. Even designer nurseries can be extreme, such as an all blue or all pink room, or a room featuring a gigantic mural of a forest or animals that engulf the space. Too much blue might make a room feel too cool, and too much pink can be too bright and active and discourage sleep, while larger-than-life murals may overwhelm a tiny baby and be overstimulating. Of course this is not to say that blue and pink or murals cannot make a wonderful nursery—it is just the extreme use of these colors or decorative elements that is not ideal. Blue, balanced with another color such as a little orange, yellow, or pink, or tempered with white, can be an excellent nursery color. And murals, if not too large or if only on one wall, can be beautiful and fun.

Balancing extremes is essential to creating a comfortable and peaceful environment. You can balance bright colors with muted, neutral tones or juxtapose plain walls with vibrant accent colors. A chair covered in a bold, patterned fabric can be balanced by adding a plain, linen pillow; balance textures by contrasting hardwood floors with a small plush area rug; balance shapes by adding a round table to a room full of square furniture. Soften sharp angles and corners by placing furniture on an angle.

Big Rooms and Small Rooms

Lofty, spacious rooms are not always inviting or cozy. If you have a very large nursery and you want it to feel more comfy, try sectioning off different areas within the room—such as a play area and a sleeping area. Use area rugs to define each space, then instead of placing furniture against the walls, position furniture around the rugs. To make a room with very high ceilings feel cozier, create a strong horizontal line around the wall no higher than eight feet. You can accomplish this by adding molding, or painting the wall up to a certain height, or installing curtain rods in line with the top of a doorframe. Consider hanging artwork lower than you might in other rooms. This will create the illusion that the room is more in proportion to your baby. Also keep in mind that painting a room with dark colors will make it feel smaller, and painting a room with lighter colors will make the space appear larger.

Your baby will most likely be comfortable in a very small room with low ceilings, but if you aren't, you can try adding lights that shine upward to help "lift" the ceiling. You could also paint the ceiling white or paint a light blue sky with clouds on the ceiling to make the room feel more open. You can also make a small room feel larger by adding a mirror that reflects a window with a nice view or beautiful artwork. A mural or work of art with a depth of field will also help "expand" the room.

Patterns and Themes

Patterns are a great way to disguise stains—and with a baby you're almost guaranteed more than a few accidents that will leave their mark. For help mixing

and matching patterns, consider the following guidelines. Choose patterns that are all in the same color family—the colors don't need to be a perfect match, but they should all mix together nicely. If you're not sure if your patterns go together then place all your fabric choices in front of you and squint your eyes. The patterns should blend together so if one fabric leaps out at you, try replacing it with another choice. Lots of really bold patterns may look too busy (and make a small room look smaller), so consider selecting only one large pattern then choosing

Small touches like this pretty patterned quilt have big impact.

one or two other smaller patterns that complement it. Also remember to balance the patterns with some empty space. A patterned pillow on a patterned chair in front of patterned wallpaper would most likely be overwhelming.

Themes are another easy, fun way to tie a room together. In addition to traditional animal, sports, and fairy-tale motifs, consider a theme based on shapes, countries, nature, or even adjectives (such as the words "soft" or "sunny"). You can also create a theme around the qualities you chose for the room, such as love and joy. Keep in mind that themes are most effective when they are not overdone. When every item in the room is part of the theme, the details get lost. So don't go overboard with your theme—there is beauty in simplicity!

Harmonious Home

Consider your home as a whole. You will create a greater feeling of harmony in your home and life if the rooms flow together. Of course each room doesn't need to be the exact same color or style, but it helps if the rooms relate to one another on some level. This includes the nursery. The nursery may have some elements that are as sophisticated as the rest of your house yet still capture the fantasy and magic of childhood. For example, you might continue the same flooring or wall colors into the nursery or you may even use the same decorating style that you use in the rest of your home. While babies haven't yet learned how the world works day-to-day, they are wise and brilliant. In the same way that you can use real words to talk to your baby, the nursery doesn't have to be the visual equivalent of "baby talk." You can save time and money by creating a room your baby can grow into—your little baby will be a "big boy" or "big girl" before you know it, and you may not want to redecorate again in just a few years.

Quick Tips

• Before you start decorating, create an inspiration board for the nursery. Begin by listing the feelings you want the nursery to evoke on the top of a large piece of thick paper. Then tape on paint samples, fabric swatches, or photos from magazines and catalogs that you like.

• Everything you place in the nursery can have meaning for you and your child, lift your spirits, and reflect your values—don't just think of what looks good, think of what feels good!

• Place a photograph of you and your partner holding your baby in view of the crib.

• If your baby has siblings, place a photo of your children all together during a happy moment in each of their rooms.

• Bring nature to the nursery by decorating with objects from nature, such as plants, or artwork of flowers and trees, or things made from natural materials like linen, cotton, wool, and solid wood.

Chapter Seven

Designing Your Life

Now that you have begun to view the decorating process as an opportunity to enhance your life, you can go one step further by using a Feng Shui tool called the Bagua Map (pronounced bah-gwa). The Bagua is an energetic map of your home and has been used in China for thousands of years to determine how the energy flow in your home affects different areas of your life. When enhancements are placed in particular areas of your home according to the Bagua Map, their positive energy is meant to produce positive changes in specific areas of your life.

The Bagua

Just as in acupuncture different parts of your body correspond to different organs, in Feng Shui different parts of your home affect different areas of your life. In Feng Shui there are nine main areas that represent your life: Helpful People, Children and Creativity, Love and Relationships, Fame and Reputation, Wealth and Prosperity, Family, Health, Knowledge and Self-Cultivation, and Career. According to the Bagua Map, each of these areas of your life directly corresponds to different areas of energy in your home. The Bagua identifies where these areas are located in your home. (See Diagram 7A.) Improving the energy in a particular area of your home results in an improvement in the corresponding life area. The Bagua Map is therefore a vessel through which you may set your intentions and manifest your dreams. When you combine your intentions with enhancements placed in these specific areas, you are using your home as a vehicle through which to design your life.

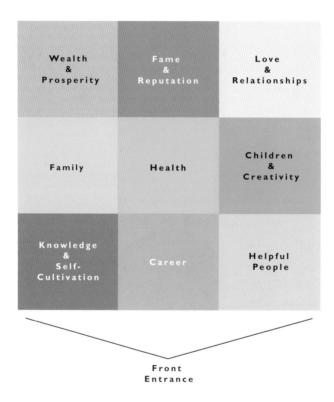

Wealth & Prosperity	Fame & Reputation	Love & Relationships
Family	Health	Children & Creativity
Knowledge & Self-Cultivation	Career	Helpful People

Front Entrance

Diagram 7A   The Bagua Map is a Feng Shui tool that shows how the energy flow in your home affects different areas of your life.

Bagua Areas

Family. This area is associated with the image of thunder. Thunder represents the voice of your ancestors from above as well as your earthly family, which includes friends who become "family." Health is an important aspect also associated with the family area. The support of your family keeps you feeling happy and healthy, and your family is who you turn to if your health is challenged. Both for a new parent and a newborn the support of family and friends is essential. Surround your baby with loving reminders that he is welcomed and supported by your immediate family, extended family, and friends. Talk to your baby and describe all the gifts that arrive from family and friends so he knows he is connected to and surrounded by the love and support of family. Also know that your child does not need to be defined by your family's history. By modeling acceptance and forgiveness for your child, he can take the best of what has come before and let go of the rest.

Wealth and Prosperity. This area is associated with the wind. It relates to material wealth, as well as other blessings including good health, family, peace, love, success, and children. Children are one of life's greatest blessings. It is through the constant cycle and movement of giving and receiving that you can activate an infinite flow of abundance in your life. The wind carries with it opportunity and new possibility. Teach your child to have a positive relationship with money and be grateful for material wealth as well as the true riches of good health, friends, and family. Celebrate and share your good fortune with gratitude.

Fame and Reputation. This area is associated with the image of fire. It concerns your reputation, including both how others think about you and how you think about yourself. Keep your child attuned to his own inner light and wisdom, so that he will always honor who he is and stay faithful to his inner values. Fan his own inner flame so that he may be true to himself and guided and enlightened by his own inner knowledge. When a person is guided by his inner light and values, he is naturally respected and admired by those around him. Lead by example by staying true to yourself, acting with integrity, and following your own inner light.

Love and Relationships. This area is associated with the image of the earth. It has to do with your relationship with others as well as with yourself. Before you can experience true love for others you must first learn to love yourself. Teach your child to have a loving, accepting, and compassionate relationship with himself. If your child is loving and kind to himself, he will be loving and kind to those around him. Children will teach you the most special kind of love:

unconditional love. Cultivate an unconditionally loving and self-forgiving relationship with yourself and others. Like the earth, your love for your child will be deep and solid. From this grounded place, you will receive, embrace, and absorb your child's expression unconditionally.

Children and Creativity. This area is associated with the image of a lake. It is about connecting to the child deep within you and your own wellspring of creativity. Children inspire us with their natural creativity and bring us true joy with their spontaneity. This area offers an opportunity to encourage your child's creativity and nurture your child's free expression, imagination, and joyful play. As you celebrate your child's full expression, unleash your own authentic creative expression. Giving birth to a child is in many ways the ultimate creative expression.

Helpful People. The helpful people area is associated with the image of the heavens. Helpful people, such as friends, family, mentors, and coworkers, may act as angels in your life. The more helpful people you have in your life, the smoother your life will flow. The heavens also remind you that there is something greater out there that is supporting you every day, whether for you this is God, a higher purpose, the energy of pure potential, spirit, nature, or your highest self. This area also relates to divine timing: being in the right place at the right time. When you live in the present moment, as all children naturally do, you are also open to all possibility. When the helpful people area is energized you feel taken care of and supported. As you take on this new role of parent and as your baby transitions into this world, it's important to feel as supported as possible; this support could mean someone handing you the right parenting book at just the right time, or friends who come over with dinner just when you feel you are too tired to cook, or a grandparent who moves in to help out. You may also wish for your children that their path be filled with loving mentors, and angels both of this world and otherworldly. Take comfort in knowing that your baby is supported beyond this physical realm.

Knowledge and Self-Cultivation. This area is associated with the mountain, and the wisdom gained from taking a higher view on life. A mountaintop perspective helps you step back and detach so you can view your life without judgment and are free to hear your inner wisdom. For babies the path of self-actualization is very clear; babies are learning and growing in every moment. Knowing that children learn by example can be a great inspiration for you to continue on your own path of self-improvement. When you are parenting your children, you may come face to face with your own issues and areas in your life that may need healing and improvement. You will be growing and learning along with your baby. This area also reminds you to be still, turn within, and take time for yourself.

Career. This area is associated with the image of water and concerns your journey through life. When you are able to align your life purpose with your work, then you have "life-work," which means your career is a calling that is connected to your life journey. As a parent, one of your jobs is to guide your child on his own unique life path. Your hope is that his journey through life, like water, will flow gently and gracefully. You may support your child in fulfilling his unique purpose, which may be very different from yours.

Health. Health is at the center of the Bagua because it is the foundation upon which you build your life. Your physical, mental, emotional, and spiritual health is essential to appreciating, experiencing, creating, and enjoying the other areas of your life. When all the Bagua areas are successfully working together, your life is healthy and balanced.

Applying the Bagua

To begin using the Bagua Map, sketch an aerial view of your home, just like a floor plan. This doesn't have to be fancy or elaborate—if your house is perfectly square your drawing would be of a simple square. If your house is L-shaped, your drawing will be in the shape of an L. If your home is two stories, start with the first story. Next draw in the inner walls, and then indicate where the front door is located. In Feng Shui, the front entrance is very important because it is where most of the energy that circulates through your home enters. Align the Career side of the Bagua Map with the wall where the front door is located—always use your home's front door even if you enter more

First Floor

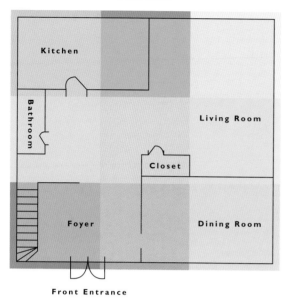

Front Entrance

Diagram 7B
Align the Knowledge and Self-Cultivation, Career, or Helpful People areas to the front door of your home and then lay the Bagua on top of your floor plan.

Second Floor

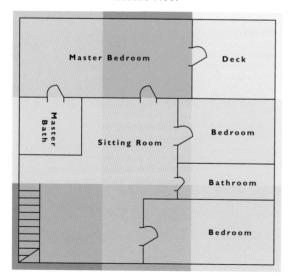

Diagram 7C

For the second floor, imagine the Bagua Map extending upward from the first floor.

Diagram 7D

In this diagram the front entrance is receded so part of the Career area is missing.

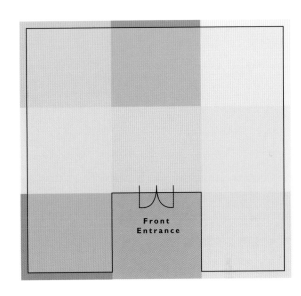

Diagram 7E

In this diagram the front entrance is receded so part of the Knowledge and Self-Cultivation area is outside the structure. In addition, all of the Wealth and Prosperity area, part of the Fame and Reputation area, and a sliver of the Family area are also missing.

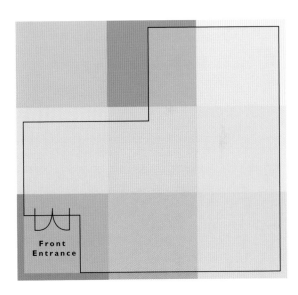

frequently through a side or garage door. The next step is to lay the Bagua Map on top of your floor plan (see Diagram 7B). The front door should be in either the Knowledge and Self-Cultivation, Career, or Helpful People area. For the second floor just imagine the map extending upward (see Diagram 7C).

"Missing" Areas

If your home is a perfect square or rectangle, it is considered a whole shape and all of the Bagua areas are within the structure (in the case of a rectangle, the Bagua Map would elongate to contain all the rooms). If your home is not a whole shape, such as an L-shape or a T-shape, chances are you have what are called missing areas. In Diagrams 7D and 7E some part of the Bagua is missing. Don't worry if you have a missing area, it can be corrected. Rather than thinking of it as missing, just know that the energy is "outside the structure of your home." To bring that energy back into your home and life, you will want to fill in that area with an enhancement. In Diagram 7F, the Love and Relationships area and some of the Fame and Reputation area are missing. You can physically fill in the area by filling in the space outside your home with landscaping, furniture, or a patio. You could also place an object like a tree or lantern in the exact corner where the edges of the house would meet if it were a complete shape. If this is not possible—for instance, if you live in an apartment on the seventeenth floor and all there is outside your home is air or if a missing area is in your neighbors' apartment—then you can energetically fill in the space using enhancements and intention. Place a mirror or artwork with depth on the wall closest to the missing area to symbolically fill in the space. If there is a window closest to the missing area, suspend a crystal in front of the window (so it reflects light) to increase and circulate the energy. (See Diagram 7F.) Oftentimes missing areas present a real opportunity for positive change because you place even more attention on enhancing them.

Diagram 7F

The tree located outside where the walls would meet if the shape were a square anchors the "missing" area. The mirror and crystal placed on the walls closest to the missing area symbolically fill in the missing space.

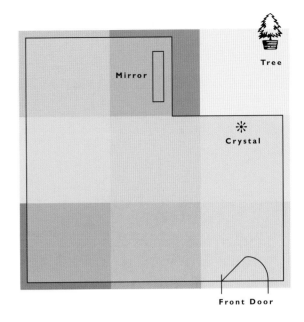

The Bagua and Your Life

Now that you know which areas of your home correspond to which areas of your life, look at your home again, this time with the understanding the Bagua Map provides. What room falls in each area and what objects do you keep in those areas? What does that room and those objects tell you about that area of your life? For example, what is in your Wealth and Prosperity area? Is there a healthy, tall, growing plant that might mean your finances are growing or is there a bathroom, which might mean your money is being flushed down the toilet? What is in your Love and Relationships area? Is your beautifully appointed master bedroom located in that area encouraging a great relationship with your partner or is there a storage closet filled with items you haven't used in years, which might mean you are neglecting your relationship? Is your Career area missing and has it been challenging to find a job or the right job? Do the things in that particular area of your home reflect the current state of affairs in the corresponding part of your life?

When you view your home from the perspective of the Bagua Map, you can appreciate the importance of keeping your home in good repair—clean, uncluttered, and filled with objects that evoke positive feelings. Each area in your home has meaning and each area is important. Most people don't have control over what room is in what area (e.g., the bathroom in Wealth and Prosperity or a storage closet in Love and Relationships), but you can improve the energy in any space by keeping it clean and uncluttered and by using enhancements.

Nursery Bagua

Now that you understand the significance of the Bagua you can apply it to the nursery. The Bagua Map may also be used on rooms individually. Draw a quick sketch of a room, in this case the nursery, and mark where the doorway entering that room is located. If there is more than one doorway, choose the door you use most often. Lay the Bagua Map over your floor plan of the room with the Career side of the Bagua Map in alignment with the wall where the door to the nursery is located. (See Diagram 7G.)

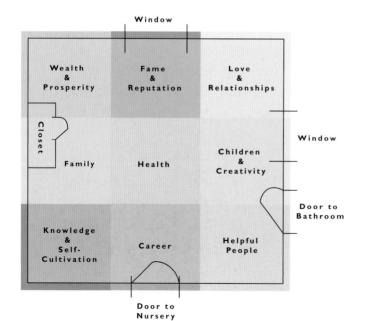

Diagram 7G

The Bagua may also be applied to individual rooms. Sketch the floor plan of the nursery and then lay the Bagua Map on top aligning the door of the nursery to the Knowledge and Self-Cultivation, Career, or Helpful People area.

If your nursery is not a perfect square or rectangle, you will need to symbolically "fill in" the missing area. In addition to the suggestions on page 112, you can also enhance the wall closest to the missing area with meaningful art, objects, or written intentions that capture the spirit of the particular area. For example, if the Knowledge and Self-Cultivation area is outside the structure, bring the knowledge energy into the room by placing knowledge enhancements such as books and learning tools in the nursery, or hanging ABC art or quotes on the wall. Square and rectangular rooms promote the greatest sense of security for a baby since there are no corners around which she can't see. To create a more balanced feel in an irregularly shaped room, you can try "squaring" it off with rugs, furniture, or a curtained wall.

Nursery Bagua Enhancements

By enhancing each part of your baby's room, you are setting the stage for your baby's success and happiness. Most people are very aware of the effect, both positive and negative, that language has on children. Yet, often people overlook the messages their environments are sending to children. The Bagua Map offers an opportunity to fill your nursery with positive messages. You may fill the room with environmental symbols that, placed in the corresponding Bagua area, will help manifest blessings and well wishes for your child. In the Family area you may place loving pictures of your family to manifest the goal of loving family bonds. In the Helpful People area you may place a picture of angels to symbolize your child always being surrounded by people who offer support and guidance. In the Children and Creativity area you may place artwork and art supplies to support your child's creative expression. Represent all the good things in life you wish for your child in the room by using the Bagua Map to anchor your intentions and well wishes. Often the best enhancements are those that have personal meaning; for example, something that may mean wealth to you but not necessarily to someone else.

The following is a list of colors and objects that can serve as enhancements

Personal photos enhance the Family area of this nursery.

for the different Bagua areas. Also included in this list is a blessing and intention to go along with each area. You can adapt these for yourself and write them out on a piece of paper and place them in the Bagua areas to serve as an enhancement or you can use them to supplement your other enhancements.

Family: Photographs of your family, hand-me-down furniture from relatives, things that are handmade from relatives, gifts from your family. Healthy plants and pictures of healthy trees and plants support the health component of this area. **Colors:** Green, blue. **Intention/Blessing:** *May you be blessed with a loving and supportive family and may you always be supported and surrounded by loving and like-minded people.*

Wealth and Prosperity: Plants, pictures of fruit-laden trees, images of water, quotes or items that signify abundance, wind chimes and mobiles that "capture the winds of fortune," crystals. **Colors:** Purple, royal blue, red. **Intention/Blessing:** *May you generously give and graciously receive an infinite flow of abundance in all its forms.*

Fame and Reputation: Lights or lamps, artwork of the sun, paintings, needlework, or letters that spell your child's name. **Colors:** Red. **Intention/Blessing:** *May your inner light always guide you and may you enjoy the recognition that comes from always following your inner light.*

Love and Relationships: Objects in pairs, anything that reminds you of love, quotes relating to unconditional love, plants, photographs of loved ones. **Colors:** White, pink, and red. **Intention/Blessing:** *May your unconditional love for yourself be reflected in wonderful relationships with others.*

Creativity and Children: Artwork, especially your artwork or (when your child's older) her artwork, handmade crafts, art materials like crayons, paper, paints, and brushes. **Colors:** Pastels such as soft pink, baby blue, pale green. **Intention/Blessing:** *May you joyously celebrate your own expression.*

Helpful People: Photographs of friends, mentors, or anyone you consider wise and helpful, pictures or statues of angels, photographs of the clouds and the sky, clocks (a clock in this area reminds you to be in the moment with your child). **Colors:** Shades of white and gray. **Intention/Blessing:** *May your life be filled with divine timing, ease, grace, and flow and may you be guided and supported by helpful people.*

Knowledge and Self-Cultivation: Pictures of mountains, lights, books or quotes by spiritual teachers, ABC art, or other learning tools. **Colors:** Dark blues and greens, black. **Intention/Blessing:** *May you fall in love with the process of learning who you are and may you realize your full potential.*

Career: Images of water, fountains, and draped, flowing fabric. **Colors:** Black. **Intention/Blessing:** *May your path be filled with grace and love and may your purpose be clear and expressed gracefully and easily through your work.*

Health: This space may be left open—clear and clean, or enhanced with a mobile, light fixture, or chandelier that incorporates the sun. **Colors:** Yellows and earth tones. **Intention/Blessing:** *May you experience a lifetime of optimal physical, mental, emotional, and spiritual health.*

Siblings can help you decorate the nursery with their artwork. This rod with clips makes rotating art easy and fun.

Quick Tips

- Lay the Bagua Map on your home and see how the different parts of your life correspond to the areas in your home.

- If any part of your life is presenting a challenge, see if anything in your home is sending you negative messages that could be intensifying the problem.

- Be sure the objects that surround your baby send a positive message.

- Use the Bagua Map as a tool to manifest positive intentions for your baby by enhancing each area.

- Write an affirmation for each area of the Bagua.

Chapter Eight

A Good Night's Sleep

One of the greatest challenges parents confront when taking care of a newborn is sleep deprivation: new parents are called upon to carry out one of life's most important jobs and often on very little sleep! You can help ease this challenge by creating a nursery designed for optimal sleep. Sleep is fundamental to ensuring your baby's health, happiness, and ability to learn and grow. Creating a sleeping sanctuary for your baby is one of the greatest things you can do to ensure your baby's well-being, and your own.

Sleep

There has been a lot of widely disseminated research on sleep in the past few years, including several excellent books about "teaching" your child how to sleep. (See Bibliography.) Sleep experts seem to agree that a "happy baby" is a well-rested baby. Books on sleep detail just how much sleep your baby needs at different ages in addition to explaining what times of day it's more natural and, therefore easier, for your child to sleep. Interestingly, the more well rested your baby, the easier it will be for him to fall asleep and stay asleep. As Dr. Weissbluth explains in his book, *Healthy Sleep Habits, Happy Child,* "It's a vicious cycle: sleep begets sleep, but sleeplessness also begets sleeplessness." The more overtired your baby is, the harder it is for him to go to sleep and stay asleep for an appropriate amount of time. Sleep deprivation accumulates over time, and, ironically, makes it more difficult for your baby to catch up. Therefore, it's best to begin practicing healthy sleeping habits with your baby right away. It's a good idea to read the sleep books before your baby is born; if you wait until after, you might be too sleep deprived and overwhelmed to digest the information!

Routine

Sleep experts suggest establishing a bedtime routine early on. Such a routine signals to your baby that it's nighttime—babies sleep so much during the day it's important to distinguish between naps and what (you hope) will be a much longer nighttime sleep. Inside the womb your baby did not distinguish day and night. In fact, while you were walking around and active during the day, your baby may have been sleeping, soothed by the motion. At night, when things were quiet and you slept, your baby may have been awake and moving.

A bedtime routine tells your baby it's time to sleep and also gives him time to unwind. A nice way to prepare babies for sleep is with a bath, followed by a story or lullaby. An important aspect of a bedtime routine is preparing the room for sleep. Ideally children's bedrooms should be used only for sleep (adult bedrooms serve two purposes: sleep and romance), and if there is anything in the room that doesn't support sleep it should be removed or put away at night. Objects that can distract a baby from sleep include toys, mobiles, and other objects designed for play. It's difficult for a baby to sleep in a room that feels "awake" and is filled with things that signal playtime to a child. Therefore, as you help your baby wind down and transition from day to night, you can transition the nursery's energy from a playroom to a sleep room. You can "cue" the room for sleep. Your bedtime routine could be as simple as cleaning up the toys and closing the curtains. The important thing is that the objects are out of sight when your baby goes to bed.

In the first months the sleeping environment will be easy to create because your baby's "view" is limited. Just being placed in a cradle, co-sleeper, or your bed is enough to cozy him in and prepare him for sleep. (Do, however, make sure that the inside of the bumper and/or sheets are not covered with active patterns or colors.) Dr. Harvey Karp in his book *The Happiest Baby on the Block* explains that many babies crave the experience of being back in the womb. Dr. Karp suggests giving your baby a "fourth trimester" by creating a "womb-like atmosphere." Having just spent the last nine months in the womb hearing your heartbeat and voice, your baby will most likely have all the comfort he needs to sleep just by being swaddled and near you. However, some babies may need a little more support to sleep well and be calm and happy. Dr. Karp's book suggests wonderful techniques for further creating the experience of being in the womb.

Eventually, as you transition to a crib for naps or nighttime, you will benefit from having already created a sleeping sanctuary. As your baby grows, he has a larger "view" of the world—which literally happens as you place your baby on his stomach versus his back and as he begins to sit up and stand up. The more

A cradle, bassinet, or co-sleeper allows you to keep your baby close.

your child can see in the nursery, the more important it is that the nursery be filled with signals indicating to your baby that it is sleep time.

Vocalizing your intentions, in a soothing "nighttime" voice, helps create a sleepy energy in the room. As you go about your routine, consider softly talking to your baby about what you're doing, by saying such things as "Now it is time to get ready for bed" and "I am going to give you a bath, close the curtains, and then put on your nightclothes" and "Next we will read and sing and after your milk it is time to sleep." You can add, "Sleep is so important for your health and it is so good for Mommy and Daddy too. We all need our sleep." As your baby gets a little older you may even be specific and say, "Now it is time for at least a two hour nap" or "I will be here if you need me, but otherwise try and sleep until seven in the morning—you will feel so good and so will Mommy and Daddy." Children understand your words long before they are capable of speaking, and they're comforted by knowing what's coming next.

You may also create a naptime routine that is a shorter and modified version of your bedtime ritual. Building in routines and rituals throughout the day helps your baby feel secure and builds trust, as over time he will see that what you say will happen next does happen next.

Sleeping Rooms and Playrooms

When you go to an amusement park, do you think about sleep? Most likely sleep is the last thing on your mind. In fact, seeing and being amongst all the rides and activities may even cause you to experience a rush of adrenaline. Yet babies' rooms are often more similar to an amusement park than they are to a restful bedroom. With the best loving intentions, many parents fill the nursery with an abundance of toys, stuffed animals, books, and games—all objects that encourage play, not sleep.

Babies are so easily stimulated and distracted that they may have a difficult time not interacting with an exciting environment. If his environment never calms down, chances are your baby will have a difficult time calming down as well. Aside from the presence of toys and games, nurseries often feature curtains, bedding, and murals depicting dancing animals, sunlit forests, or moving cars and trucks. Keep in mind that animals that are awake will never shut their eyes, it will never be nighttime in that sunlit forest and racing cars will never stop moving.

It's helpful to think of a playroom and a sleeping room as two separate things, and ideally you'll create separate areas for each. Try to gear the nursery toward restful activities such as sleeping, dressing, and nursing and to define other distinct areas in different rooms in your home as play areas. One benefit to this arrangement is that as your child gets older, you will not be tied to playing with him in his room. If you define a play area in the kitchen, for example, you can keep an eye on your child as you cook; if you do so in your family room, you can watch your child while you return e-mails, pay bills, work, or just relax.

If you'd like your nursery to be both a sleep room and playroom, it's best to define separate sleep and play areas. You can do this with furniture or curtains, using the latter as "screens" to close off the play area from the crib. If your nursery is too small to section off, then keep in mind that you can also have a nap or bedtime routine that includes changing the nursery from play mode to sleep mode. When you select furniture and storage systems, choose cabinets with doors or bins with lids to hide toys at night.

The following list gives you some things to consider as you create a peaceful nursery.

Art. Art can have a powerful effect on you, particularly what you see first and last upon waking and going to sleep. If your child can see the artwork from the crib, make sure it is peaceful and encourages sleep.

Mobiles and objects over the crib. Large, heavy mobiles are best placed over a changing table. Can you imagine waking up in the middle of the night and having something hanging over your head that is almost as big as you are? If your baby's crib becomes a play area, detach the swinging portion of the mobile each night and leave the clamp on the crib rail. You should also remove heavy artwork from above the crib. Ceiling fans with sharp blades send out extreme energy and are disruptive to sleep. In addition, the dust that accumulates on the fan is then circulated into the air, which does not contribute to a healthy environment. Be sure the crib is not directly underneath the fan and clean the dust off frequently. If you don't need the fan, you can replace it with a light.

Murals. You cannot easily change a mural so check to see that the image portrayed is in alignment with sleep. Also keep in mind that large looming figures can be overwhelming to a baby, and if the mural portrays active figures, they keep the room energized, even at bedtime. If you do choose an active mural, consider curtaining it off at night.

Toys. The key with toys in a sleeping room is to make sure you can put them away. Have plenty of easy-to-use storage areas like cabinets, closets, baskets, and bins so you can easily and quickly transform the room. Bins and baskets are particularly easy because you can just throw all the toys inside, and even young children will enjoy putting things inside them.

Colors. In Chapter Three we discussed the effect colors have on your mind and body. It is best to paint the room in a color that is somewhat neutral and conducive to sleep. Use the more active and awake colors for accents, or in an area that cannot be seen from the crib. You can always "wake up" the room for playtime with brightly colored toys, but it's difficult to quiet down orange walls.

Mirrors. Mirrors have active energy and are therefore great enhancements. However, in the bedroom, this active energy is not conducive to sleep. So choose a small to medium size mirror and place it where it won't reflect your sleeping baby.

View from the crib. What you see last before falling asleep and first upon waking creates a very powerful impression. Keep the views from the crib peaceful and calming.

Televisions. Televisions have a very lively energy even when they're turned off. To ensure a good night's sleep, it is best not to have a television in your baby's room. If you choose to have a stereo, place it in a cabinet with doors that can hide it at night, and keep it away from the crib.

Crib placement. Placing the crib so that your baby has a view of the door, the Command Position (see page 38), will encourage a peaceful night's sleep.

Placing toys away in a chest or basket at night turns a nursery from a playroom to a sleep room.

You can further support your baby by placing one side of the crib against a solid wall, which will give your baby a greater feeling of security.

Sharp angles. Check to make sure there are no sharp corners pointing toward your baby as he sleeps. For example, if you have a table by the crib or nursing chair, it is better to choose one with rounded edges, or one that is circular. Sharp corners send out sharp energy, and people are simply not as comfortable sitting in front of a sharp edge as they would be in front of a gentle curve. If a wall protrudes near a crib with a sharp angle, you can soften the corner by covering it with a plant, hanging a banner or mobile in front of it, or draping a fabric curtain along the edge.

Sheets and bumpers. Make sure the inside of your bumper and your sheets are either solid colors or feature patterns that are restful. Bright sheets or sheets covered with action figures or "awake" characters are too stimulating and will not help your baby get a good night's rest.

Clutter. Clutter stagnates energy in a room. To ensure a good night's rest, make sure everything is picked up before bedtime and don't store things under the bed. You will probably need to clutter clear the room periodically. Just making more space gets the energy flowing again and can help children sleep better. A baby, like an adult, thrives in a peaceful, clutter-free environment.

Light

Lighting is a very important cue for sleep. Your biological clock is set by light. You will want to be able to darken the nursery to help your baby sleep. Although in the winter you might want your baby to wake up to the sun, in the spring and summer, when the sun and birds are up at five thirty A.M., you will not want your baby getting up too. Make sure your curtains are dark enough to eliminate unwanted light. If they aren't, consider getting them lined or installing dark shades. The ideal situation is to have a variety of lighting choices. You can install a dimmer switch or simply use lamps with bulbs of differing wattage.

Dimming the lights during the bedtime ritual is a wonderful cue for your baby to prepare both mentally and physically for sleep.

Sound

A quiet environment is also important to help your baby sleep, particularly as he gets older and is stimulated by every little noise. Locating your nursery in a quiet part of your home is helpful. White noise machines can mask unwanted noise that may keep your baby awake, like a dog barking or your neighbors talking. In addition, white noise machines mimic the sounds your baby heard while in the womb and may help lull your baby to sleep. If you use a white noise machine, place it away from your baby's crib to avoid the effect of EMFs.

Energy Cleansing

At nighttime you will want your child surrounded by things that have a quiet energy. Energy cleansing involves shifting the unseen energy in a room. If your child has been playing in the nursery all day, even when the toys are picked up and out of sight the room will still be filled with playful energy. It is similar to how a room feels after a party: the guests may be gone, but the party energy lives on. After picking up your child's toys, you may wish to open the windows for a few moments to "clear the air." If your child has had several sleepless nights, there is a greater chance of another sleepless night because the energy is holding that pattern in place. Often you can break the cycle by doing a simple energy cleansing. Open the windows and mist the room with water to break the sleepless energy pattern. Or simply wash the sheets and then, while remaking the crib, set a positive intention for a good night's sleep.

Receiving Help

Unlike other big events in life such as a wedding, after you give birth you don't get a honeymoon period to rest and recover—the work begins immediately and it's pretty much around the clock. It's important to get as much sleep as you possibly can for the first few months, and friends and family can be an enormous help. Once you can use a breast pump, or if you are bottle-feeding, friends or family may be willing to give you a break once in a while and do some night feedings. If there is a grandparent who is willing to help out, by all means accept the offer. Your parents will likely remember the basics of taking care of a baby, and one thing they're very practiced in is taking care of you, which in turn will help you take care of your baby.

You may choose to hire a doula or night nurse for the first few weeks. Doulas and night nurses are professionals who live with newborns day in and day out. They will help get you and your baby on the right track by teaching you a variety of ways to handle the night feedings that will work best for you and your partner. Also take advantage of the nurses at the hospital. One of the most important things a professional will teach you to do is swaddle your baby. Babies have gotten used to the small environment of your womb, and swaddling a baby helps re-create this feeling of security and immobility.

Your partner will also be a great support. Before your child is born, discuss what expectations you will have of each other in this area. Will you share the night feedings? If your partner is working and you are not, will you handle the feedings alone, so your partner may be rested for work and better able to help out in the evenings? Will your partner take some time off from work to do some night feedings so you can rest and heal? Will you share the feedings if and when you are both working? Since it is advisable that someone sleeps near or in the same room as the baby for the first six months, decide if you will have the bassinet in your room, or if you will sleep in your baby's room so your partner sleeps undisturbed. If you're nursing, your partner can help out by bringing the baby to you in bed (if your baby is not already in bed) and changing the diaper. You will want to conserve as much energy as possible, particularly if

you're recovering from the birth or breast-feeding.

One of the best things you can do for yourself, which almost every mother advises, is to sleep when your baby sleeps. With all the excitement and things to do, this is often hard advice to follow, but remember that the more behind you get on sleep, the harder it is to catch up and the less effective you will be when taking care of your child. By taking care of yourself, it will be much easier to take care of your child. Everyday tasks, such as sending e-mails, making phone calls, and running errands, may be difficult to accomplish as you adjust to life with a newborn. This is a special time and it goes very quickly, so try to let go of the tasks and enjoy the moment. Rest assured that the time will come when your baby is sleeping through the night and you will get back to your usual routine. However, if you get too sleep deprived, when that time comes, you will be too tired to accomplish anything or even enjoy your free time.

You can also support yourself with a positive attitude. "Reframing" is a technique that involves changing your perception about a particular circumstance. Dr. Jay Gordon, a pediatrician and author of *Listening to Your Baby,* encourages parents to "reframe" by telling a wonderful story about a couple who kept insisting that their newborn was sleeping through the night. Dr. Gordon could not understand how a newborn could sleep all night without waking up to eat. Upon further questioning, the couple explained, "Well, she does wake up to eat three times, but then she goes right back to sleep." This shift in perception allowed the couple to feel that they were sleeping all night. And you will sleep too, just not in the way you are used to sleeping. Our minds have a powerful effect on how we look at a situation. You can feel more rested by acknowledging the sleep you do get. It's easy after months of not sleeping to feel tired because you are so used to *thinking* you are sleep deprived.

Adult Bedrooms

Take some time to focus on your bedroom. You must first nurture yourself before you can nurture another. So in the spirit of self-nurturing and to support your marriage or partnership, be sure to create a comfortable, cozy, and romantic bedroom.

Adult bedrooms should serve only two purposes: rest and romance. Unfortunately, in today's busy world people are constantly multi-tasking, and so are their bedrooms. Frequently bedrooms also serve as home offices, exercise rooms, and TV rooms. Computers, desks, televisions, and exercise equipment all have very active energy and are constantly calling out for our attention. Imagine how hard it is to have a restful night's sleep when you're staring at a visual to-do list of work that needs to be completed, bills that need to be paid, or an exercise routine that needs to be started. If possible, move anything that does not support sleep or sex to another room. This includes keeping your children's toys out of the bedroom. If this is not possible, conceal these objects when they are not in use: hide the TV in an armoire or closet, or simply cover it with a piece of fabric at night. Try hiding exercise equipment or a desk behind a screen. During the day the screen can sit in a corner as a decorative piece and at night can be pulled out to conceal your work/exercise area.

In addition to having a very active energy, electronics generate electric and magnetic fields (EMFs), which may potentially cause serious health problems. Research about the negative health effects of EMFs is ongoing and not yet conclusive, but there is no doubt that the growing use of computers, cell phones, microwaves, and other household appliances have significantly increased our exposure to EMFs. Since you spend so much time in bed, this is an excellent opportunity to give your body a break from this exposure by removing as much electronic equipment from around the bed as possible. In addition to televisions and computers, this includes smaller appliances such as digital clocks, radios, and cell phone chargers. Try replacing your digital clock with a battery operated clock or move these items as far away from the bed as possible—for example on a dresser across the room.

For many couples it's hard to be romantic when you are both exhausted from night feedings. To encourage more romance in your life, decorate the bedroom with sensual colors, including skin tones, like beige and chocolate, or use shades of red, the color associated with passion, like burgundy and terra-cotta. Keep in mind that a bright red may be too active for the bedroom and could potentially make sleep difficult. Add something to the room that says romance to you—such as candles, music, or artwork. Also try removing photographs of your friends, family, and children from around the bed, or from the bedroom entirely. You don't need to be reminded of your mother-in-law or even your new baby during a romantic moment with your spouse. Instead, hang a photograph of you and your partner that reminds you both of a happy moment that you shared together. At a time when your relationship may be under the strain of adjusting to new circumstances, it is nice to remember all the good times you've had together.

Place your bed in the Command Position of the room, with the support of a solid wall and headboard behind you. Make sure that both you and your partner have a view of the door, but that your feet are not pointed directly at the door. Ideally, neither partner will have a direct view into the bathroom. In Feng Shui, bathrooms are places where energy goes down and out the drains and can be a "drain" on your health. If you do have a view of a bathroom, keep the bathroom door closed at night.

Be sure that you and your spouse each have a side table of approximately equal size. One side table, or side tables of substantially different sizes, creates a sense of inequality between partners.

You will spend almost a third of your life asleep in bed, so make sure your bed is a healthy place. According to Environmental Consultant and certified Bau-Biologist Mary Cordaro, "For those who have allergies, asthma, chemical sensitivities, or frequent colds and flu, a healthy, natural bedroom free of pollutants may not only give you relief, but also provide a big boost to your immune system. For the healthy person, the healthy bedroom is pure prevention for those of all ages, and most importantly for children, whose developing bodies are much more vulnerable." Just like your baby, your health will be supported by natural bedding. Next time you purchase a new bed, consider buying a mattress made of wool. (See Resources.) Until then you could buy a wool mattress pad to cover the mattress you do have. Wool is a versatile material that can help you maintain a comfortable body temperature all year round, in both warm and cool climates; it also wicks away moisture, resists mold, mildew, and dust mites and is naturally flame resistant. Also, replace sheets and pillows made of synthetic materials, and be particularly wary of permanent press materials that often contain formaldehyde. In addition to containing chemicals, synthetic materials don't breathe and therefore trap moisture that can lead to mold and mildew, which can trigger allergies. Try natural materials that breathe, like linen, or organically grown cotton sheets, and wool blankets. Mattresses also attract dust mites, which can trigger or inflame allergies and asthma, so you might consider sealing your mattress in an allergy cover made from natural materials to create a barrier between you and the dust mites. You can wash the allergy cover to keep the dust mites off.

Quick Tips

• Read parenting books that discuss sleep before your baby is born, so you will be prepared to establish healthy sleep patterns early on. Discuss with your partner before your baby is born your expectations of each other regarding night feedings.

• Establish a routine that you and your baby will follow every night to indicate that it is bedtime.

• Each night, turn the nursery from a playroom to a sleep room by removing active items such as toys and mobiles. Placing these items in storage containers or closets can become part of the nighttime routine. Make sure the art, walls, sheets, and views from the crib all support a peaceful night's sleep.

• Place the crib in the Command Position so your baby has a view of the door and a solid wall behind him.

• Be sure your own bedroom supports rest and romance by removing or hiding things like televisions, computers, exercise equipment, or any other distractions. Support your relationship by creating a sensual room filled with warm colors, candles, inviting fabrics, and a happy picture of you and your partner.

• Good sleep is essential for good health. Create a chemical and dust-free sleeping environment by using natural cotton sheets, wool blankets, and allergy covers.

• Remember to sleep when your baby sleeps!

Chapter Nine

Preparing Yourself

You have set your intentions and filled the process of creating a nursery with love and purpose. Now enjoy the end of your pregnancy. Spend time with yourself while your baby is still in the womb. Also spend time with your partner, have special days with your older children, visit with friends, and rest. Finally, enjoy the home you have prepared—cook family dinners, light candles, buy flowers, invite friends over, and spend time in the nursery you have created. Don't let the nursery sit untouched—bring positive energy to the space by visiting daily and opening windows to let in fresh air.

Deciding You're Ready

It's best to have your home ready at least one month before your baby is due. Even if you haven't accomplished everything you'd planned on, let go and declare it done. By deciding you're finished a month in advance, you'll have time to rest and take care of yourself before your baby arrives; and if your baby comes early, you'll be prepared. Expectant parents often get anxious about when their baby will be born. This is an experience you can prepare for but cannot control. Surrender to the unknown and accept that you may not be able to plan the day your baby arrives. Once your baby is born you'll need to learn to let go of plans and surrender to your child's needs anyway. So begin practicing now by letting go of plans and deciding that you and your home are ready, even if there are still some things on your to-do list.

If your religion or belief system does not support setting up your nursery in advance, then focus on preparing the rest of your home before your baby is born. Perhaps you can even prepare the room itself by painting and cleaning. You can also consider registering for the things you will need and ordering the furniture and essentials a few months in advance, but wait to pick them up or have them delivered until after the baby is born. If you do wait, it will be particularly important for you to have help from friends and family. A month before your due date, plan how the nursery will be set up and who will do it. Give this person a key to your home and explain how you would like things arranged. When you begin labor, call this person so they can start picking things up, receiving deliveries, opening boxes, washing linens and clothes, and even reading instructions so they can show you how to work things. If you're delivering in a hospital, arrange to have the nursery prepared while you are still in the hospital.

Gratitude

It is natural to experience some anxiety as you anticipate the birth of your baby and prepare for such a huge life change. But the stress caused by fear is unpleasant, not good for your health, not good for those around you, and not good for the baby inside you. One of the best tools for letting go of fear and de-stressing is to express gratitude, which shifts us from a place of fear to a place of love. In his book *What Happy People Know*, Dan Baker explains that it is actually physiologically impossible for your body to hold the feelings of fear and appreciation at the same time. Try creating a mental list of everything you are grateful for in your life the moment you feel stress. For example, if you are stuck in traffic that is making you late for an important meeting and you feel anxious or stressed, stop yourself from focusing on the traffic, then step back from the situation and begin thinking of all the blessings in your life, such as good health, food, friends, and family, and the gift of expecting a baby. You will instantly move out of a stressful state and have a clearer perspective on life. The more you practice, the easier it will be to move to this state when facing a greater challenge.

Expressing gratitude for all the blessings in your life can become a daily practice. Each night before bed you can make a written, verbal, or mental list of all the things that you are grateful for in your life. Include a few things on the list that happened that day, no matter how challenging your day may have been. Remember, like attracts like. Usually the things you are grateful for tend to multiply in your life. Your thoughts are made up of energy, so the more you think about something, the more energy you give it and the more quickly it will manifest. Focus on positive experiences and let go of the rest. For example, if you know someone who had an easy delivery, focus on that knowledge and be grateful that it's possible for you to have an easy delivery as well. Learn about as many positive birth experiences as you can. If you catch yourself thinking negative thoughts or getting wrapped up in a negative fantasy, stop yourself in the moment and ask, "Do I

Placing visual reminders of your hopes and goals in your home inspires you to realize your dreams.

really want to create this for myself?" Then firmly respond, "No, I am letting that go. Instead, I choose this . . ." and create a joyful vision. You can control your imagination, so why not imagine constructive visions?

Self-Nurturing

There is an expression that in order to love another you must first learn to love yourself. If you are feeling drained or are low on energy, how can you possibly love and nurture another? You can't. Pregnancy is the perfect example, because your baby's survival is dependent on your own. Your baby is affected by the food you eat and how much rest you've had. Some research shows that the baby is even affected by your emotions. If you are feeling stressed, the baby will feel stressed. So by taking care of yourself, you're taking care of the baby. The same is true after your baby is born: many new parents feel selfish taking time to care for themselves, but it is important to realize that as much as you want a healthy and happy baby, your baby wants a healthy and happy parent. It can be challenging to find time for yourself, but it is very important for your well-being and your child's.

Your love for your child will be so strong that it will be natural to want to give all of yourself to your baby. While the elation of being a new parent and your love for your child will allow you to do so for a short period of time, it will be impossible to sustain that level of self-sacrifice for too long: your energy will get depleted and you will experience burnout. Unlike crunching for an exam or a big presentation and then crashing the day after to recover, your child is dependent on you around the clock, seven days a week, so if you deplete yourself you won't ever have the luxury of a recovery period. Make a habit of giving back to yourself each day in whatever way you can. Daily, easy, and quick self-care rituals are the most effective over time. Below is a list of some things to do for yourself every day:

- Have a cup of tea alone.
- Take a walk.

- Lie on your back for three to ten minutes and focus on your breathing.
- Take a bubble bath.
- Read a chapter of a book.
- Take a twenty-minute nap.
- Soak your feet for ten minutes in warm water.
- Exercise or take a yoga class.

Whatever you choose to do, make it all about you. Know that the state of your health and well-being influences your child's well-being. You have learned how to make a home that boosts and lifts your energy, but it is equally important to nurture your mind, body, and spirit. You may do this by maintaining a healthy body, thinking positive thoughts, letting emotions flow freely, and connecting to a higher purpose. Some great simple ways to lift your energy are: eating healthy meals, exercising, spending time with friends, spending time in nature, laughing, meditating, dancing, and doing things you love.

Being the Most of Who You Are

Children help us to know ourselves—they are little mimics and pick up everything they see. You can see your words and actions reflected back to you as you watch your child. As a parent, remember that your child is observing you and learning from you in every moment and that one of the best gifts you can give him is to be the most of who you are. When you see yourself through your child's eyes, you'll be inspired to be the best you can be.

However, keep in mind there is no such thing as a perfect person, home, or parent. Your loving and clear intention is what really counts. As a parent you will be called upon to make choices again and again. The important thing is to be mindful of the impact of your choices and to trust yourself and honor your intuition. There are no perfect parents, so try not to judge yourself if you slip into old patterns or do something you feel is less than ideal. You will have many more opportunities for improvement!

Often pregnancy and parenting remind us of our own parents' strengths and weaknesses. You have the opportunity to let go of any emotional baggage so that you don't pass it on to your child. Celebrate and emulate the things your parents did that worked and let go of the things that you feel may not have worked. The best way to release your parents' patterns and not take them on as your own is through a process of forgiveness. You too will most likely make mistakes along the way, but in life our imperfections make us human, so let go of your judgments and treat others and yourself with compassion and love. Learn from mistakes and then forgive your parents or yourself and let go of them. The following is a step-by-step process to release judgments:

1. Set aside some uninterrupted time.

2. Set an intention that through this process these judgments will be released and ask that any healing or clearing for your highest good and the highest good of your baby take place now with ease.

3. Write down on a piece of paper any negative feelings, grudges, resentments, or judgments you may be holding.

4. Move through this process quickly.

5. Once you have completed the process, burn the paper in a safe place. Burning the paper symbolizes releasing your judgments.

As you begin parenting your child, you also have the opportunity to re-parent yourself. Set the intention that as you care for your baby, you are caring for yourself. Simply setting that intention will allow you to benefit from all the loving energy that you're directing toward your baby.

Building a Relationship with Your Baby

A great way to create a strong foundation for a positive relationship with your baby is to start communicating when your baby is in the womb. From about the fifth month of pregnancy, your baby will be able to hear your voice. Even before your baby understands your words, she can certainly "hear" your love and understand your intentions—she is tuned in to your behavior, feelings, and energy in the womb and from the moment she is born. Babies have an ability to understand language much earlier than they are capable of speaking it. So begin speaking to your baby every day, assuming she understands your every word. By starting to communicate this early, you will have already begun a relationship with your baby before she is even born, making your transition into parenthood and your baby's transition into the world that much easier.

In the womb your baby will be responding to you with kicks and movement. Let your baby know that you're listening. When she gets your attention with a kick, respond by saying something like "Hello, sweet baby." You can also respond by giving your belly a rub. After your prenatal checkups, let her know that everything is okay. You may say to your baby, "You are so healthy and strong. You are growing perfectly." Your baby is listening, so use this time to share as many positive ideas as possible such as:

> *Your mommy and daddy love you and always will.*
>
> *You have so many friends and family who are here to support you and can't wait to meet you.*
>
> *You are going to love your home and your life.*
>
> *You are healthy and strong.*
>
> *I will always love and respect you and be honest with you, and you will always love and respect me and be honest with me.*
>
> *I know this birth experience will be amazing.*

After your baby is born, it will be natural to continue this communication. You will already know your baby and have had the benefit of a nine-month relationship. If you are adopting your baby or if someone else is carrying your child for you, try writing to your baby in a journal. Communicate with your baby by writing down all the wonderful thoughts and feelings you're having in anticipation of his arrival. Once the baby has arrived in your home, you can read a page from your journal to him every night.

Imagine being a baby in a totally new world, completely dependent on someone else and with limited means of communication. The more you can treat your newborn with the care, love, and respect with which you would want to be treated, the more that same care, love, and respect will be given back to you as she grows. One way of establishing this kind of conscious parenting is by assuming your baby understands everything you say. Let her know everything you are doing. Imagine how you would feel if you were picked up abruptly, placed in water, or disrobed? Say to her, "I am going to pick you up now. Now we are going to take a bath," and so forth. The more honest and clear your communication with your baby, the more you will build trust, which is at the core of any good relationship. You may also welcome your baby into her new environment by giving her a tour of your house. Explain to her "this is your room. This is the stuffed animal that I had when I was little. This is your blanket that Grandma made for you." Exploring your home together is a wonderful way to entertain your baby.

Being in the Moment

You have prepared a special welcome—through your home and through your loving intentions—and it is now important to slow down so you may fully experience the unfolding miracle. These days things seem to move very quickly— we're connected at all moments by phones, e-mail, and instant messaging, enabling us to work, socialize, and take care of a newborn all at the same time. Having a newborn provides you with an opportunity to learn from your baby how to live simply and be in the moment. Babies are about being, not doing, and the more you can let go and be in the present moment, the easier and more enjoyable the process of raising your child will be. Babies do not think about finishing their milk quickly because they have something to do, or about waking up from their nap early because they have somewhere to go. A fast-paced lifestyle does not fit with a baby's schedule—or more accurately, lack of schedule. Babies do not think that anything is more important than what is right in front of them, which is a very loving and respectful way to live. Give your child the same focused attention he gives you.

After your baby is born, your priorities will change, and parenting will become one of the most meaningful jobs you will ever have. Things that used to feel important may not seem as important anymore. In the context of caring for your baby, everything on your to-do list can wait. How many times in life will you have this special time with your infant? Know that being with your baby is the most important thing you can do.

You have simplified your home and life so that you may have more time for your baby. Now enjoy the time—simply. Taking care of a newborn offers a unique opportunity to let go of time and consciously go about your daily routines with a sense of purpose. The day's big events for a baby are eating, sleeping, bathing, getting dressed, going for a walk, and perhaps seeing a visitor. It will be necessary for you to slow down to appreciate these little moments, to make sure that each is filled with love, meaning, and fun. Your baby may nurse and then fall asleep in your arms, so take the phone off the hook and enjoy the slow pace of life for a change. You can create more time to spend with your baby by reevaluating your priorities. Even evaluate the things you do for your children. For example, instead of taking hours and hours to plan a fancy birthday party, plan a low-key party and enjoy the extra time to play with your child. Children live in the moment; for children the only time is now, and the frazzled week that you spent preparing for a celebration may, in a child's eyes, not be worth the ultimate payoff of the event.

The Forty Days

A woman who has just given birth will need time to heal her body and adjust to this huge life change. Many women feel pressure to do it all—and most likely a woman can do it all—but is this what's best for her? This is a very personal question that only she can answer. Her body has been through a lot, and she may need to give herself the time to heal. A woman who takes the time to care for herself immediately after the birth will probably regain her full strength faster than a woman who pushes herself to do too much before she is ready.

One way for a new mother to regain her strength is to allow herself forty days to rest and recuperate after the birth. Forty days is a spiritually significant time period. In addition, most doctors will tell a woman that it takes up to six weeks for her body to heal. The Sikh religion has a custom called "the forty days," which supports both the mother and baby, physically and spiritually, after the birth. The traditional Sikh custom holds that the mother should not be farther than nine feet from her baby and not receive any visitors for forty days. You may wish to create your own interpretation of "the forty days." For example, the mother and baby could stay primarily in the home for the first forty days, after which it's believed that the mother has most likely healed physically and the baby is now ready to venture out beyond its second womb, the home. If a woman doesn't allow herself time to heal and adjust, the healing process can take much longer. If you stay at home with your baby, you can rest whenever your baby sleeps. In her book, *Bountiful, Beautiful, Blissful,* yoga teacher and Sikh Gurmukh explains, "It is good to sleep when the baby sleeps, because otherwise it can take up to two and a half years to regain your full strength rather than a mere forty days." Even if mother and child cannot or do not want to stay at home for all forty days, keeping this time period in mind encourages mothers to slow down, rest, rejuvenate, heal, and reflect on the intensity of what they have just experienced.

You don't need to be superwoman—running errands, working full-time, going to parties, and socializing immediately after giving birth. However, if you are ready to resume your "normal" life and think that it will help you adjust to parenting better, then by all means do what you think is best, but first give your-self permission to take as much time as you can to do what you need to do to take care of yourself.

Asking for Help

There is a great deal of truth to the expression, "It takes a village to raise a child." Parenting is often challenging, and it is important to receive the support of family, friends, home, and communities. Get in the habit now of asking for help from family and friends. If you, like many people, live far away from your family and don't have the support of a strong community, create a family of like-minded people. Find a community of expecting parents, perhaps by join-ing a prenatal yoga class, or by attending birthing classes. It's wonderful to be around other people experiencing what you are experiencing so you can ask questions and share thoughts. Especially after your baby is born, you will want support. Often new parents are overwhelmed with the many emotions that ac-company the birth of a baby. Unfortunately because parents sometimes feel guilty about feeling anything other than joy, they do not share their feelings with others and therefore rob themselves of the support they may receive from friends and family. Take the risk and share your thoughts, you will eventually find someone who has had a similar experience to yours and you will most likely feel better by simply realizing you're not alone.

This is a great time to sign up for a parenting class. Find a class that is orga-nized by age. This way you have playmates for your baby and you have the bene-fit of sharing experiences with other parents who are going through the exact same stage as you are. Children change so quickly month to month and between sleep deprivation and "nursing brain" you will find that most parents—even those whose children are just a few months older than yours will have already forgotten what went on in that particular stage.

You'll also need your partner and friends to remind you to find the humor in parenting. A sense of humor can help you transcend the small aggravations.

In a single moment, humor can shift the energy of a situation and give you a different perspective. From this new perspective, it's often much easier to be patient when dealing with frustrations or new challenges. Another way to shift your perspective is to not take things personally. Sometimes your baby is upset just because she's upset, not because you're doing anything wrong. It's much easier to be patient during a challenging moment if you're not judging yourself. Instead of getting caught up in the moment, look at it as a challenge. Be creative and try to figure out what's bothering your child. Remember that your baby is on your side. You may say something such as, "I hear how upset you are and I am going to do whatever I can to figure out how I can help you." Asking advice from friends, reading a parenting book, or even just taking a moment to breathe may give you more clarity about the situation.

You may also ask for help from a higher power. For each individual this will be something different. You may ask for help from God, Mother Nature, spirit, the universe, guardian angels, your higher-self, or whatever feels right to you. Asking for help is a wonderful act of self-nurturing. A great way to begin your day is to take a few breaths, close your eyes, and send positive energy toward your day. You may say, silently or aloud, "I ask that this day be filled with light, love, grace, ease, and flow. I ask for assistance and send light to this day. I surrender this day to you to guide and flow through me and inspire me moment to moment." You will be amazed at how your day may flow when you feel supported.

Your Partner and Expectations

Experienced parents will often say to expectant parents "children change everything." And they're right. You will change, your priorities will shift, your perceptions about the world will change, and your relationship will change. A new person is about to enter your relationship—it *will* be different. You and your partner won't have the same amount of time together or the freedom you're accustomed to and in all likelihood you won't be getting as much rest as you are now. Depending on your delivery and if you're nursing, your physical relationship with your partner might change too. To ensure that the changes in your relationship that could accompany your newborn are positive, and that your relationship grows stronger, it helps to discuss with your partner before the baby is born what your expectations are of each other. Talk with each other about how you think your lifestyle might change and how you'll handle any challenges that could arise.

Discussing your expectations helps alleviate any pressure you may put on yourselves that you "should" be doing something. For instance, as you adjust to the demands of caring for a newborn, you may not have a home-cooked meal on the table every night or the house may be a little messier than normal, so it might be helpful if you and your partner have agreed in advance that takeout and a little mess is acceptable for a time. You'll feel more at peace if there isn't a part of you that feels inadequate or let down when you or your partner don't have time to make dinner or pick up the house. You also might want to discuss how your roles may change. If you've made a choice to spend a few weeks in the house resting, allowing your body to heal, and taking care of your newborn, it helps if your partner knows that during this time he may be taking on extra re-sponsibilities, such as paying bills and making all the meals. This way you can enjoy the time without feeling guilty. Often it is unrealistic expectations, guilt, and judgments that disrupt the relationship more than the actual circumstances.

In the same way that taking care of yourself is essential to caring for your baby, taking care of your relationship is also important. Your child will want happy parents. If you both discuss in advance that the majority of your free time together will be spent enjoying your baby, it will alleviate any feelings that you're not doing enough for each other. However, it's also important to estab-lish some private time together early on. One date night a week can go a long way. Even taking time to light candles and sit down to dinner together each night or going to bed half an hour later than you planned so you can talk about your day is important to keeping the part of your relationship that does not involve your baby intact. One of the most important gifts you can give your baby and yourself is to have a loving relationship with your partner. Model for your child how to be in a healthy relationship. It's difficult to imagine now, but eventually your baby will grow up and have his own relationship and family, and when that time comes you'll be very grateful to have preserved and nurtured a vibrant, loving relationship with your partner.

As you discuss your future together as new parents, it's helpful to keep in mind that many of the changes you're about to experience won't last forever. Don't be upset if your relationship goes through an adjustment period. Often parents panic thinking the first few months of having a new baby at home is how life will be forever. Fortunately, this is not the case; as your baby gets older you will sleep more, you will have more personal time, and you will experience intimacy the way you did pre-baby. It will get easier with each day.

Everything Changes

The cliché "enjoy them while they're babies, it goes so fast" is only too true. Children grow and change before your eyes. It is important to embrace change by continuously reflecting it in your environment. Nowhere is this more obvious than in children's spaces. It makes sense that your nursery will adapt to meet the evolving needs of your growing baby. For instance, just look at your crib: as your baby grows, the mattress will be lowered and then the crib converted into or replaced by a toddler bed.

You will want to build your newborn's sense of security by making only small changes to his room, since radical changes in the first year may be overwhelming for him. Constant clutter clearing is a great way to keep the energy moving, and it doesn't change the room too drastically. Children are always outgrowing clothes and toys, so plan on storing, donating, throwing away, or giving away, on a monthly basis, whatever your child no longer needs. By clutter clearing regularly, you're not only adapting the room as your child grows, but also renewing and refreshing the energy in it.

As your child gets older, you'll realize that what may have been positive for you and your baby last year may not be any longer. If something doesn't seem right anymore, like the position of the crib or the enhancements, make a change. If you embrace change and learn to change with it, to "go with the flow," your life will transform in a graceful and magical way.

Role of Parent and Maker of Homes

In our culture we often focus on the big events, such as weddings, parties, graduations, promotions, holidays, and other dramatic events. While these occasions yield great memories and carry on important customs, they are rare, isolated, and brief moments in time. It is important to focus on your everyday life—the small moments and daily rituals that comprise the majority of time you spend on the planet. Each moment of your day, from getting dressed, to cooking a meal, to talking on the phone, to holding your baby may be filled with art and beauty. Embrace and redefine the role of "homemaker." A homemaker may be a single person, a parent, a couple, or a family. You may be a homemaker whether you work outside of the home or not. Think of a homemaker as a maker of homes. Each day offers you an opportunity to celebrate and be grateful for the blessings in your life.

Raising kind, empathic children, who love and accept themselves and others, is one of the greatest contributions you can make in today's world. Creating peace within yourself, your children, and your home is a first step to creating peace in the world. The feeling of peace your children feel at home is a feeling they can take with them, wherever they go.

Quick Tips

- If possible, slow down during your last month of pregnancy: take time to rest and enjoy time with your partner. Celebrate your peaceful home and spend time in the nursery.

- Make a commitment to daily self-care. Set aside time every day to nurture yourself. This may mean five uninterrupted minutes to enjoy a cup of tea, or an hour to take a walk in nature. Whatever you choose, commit to doing it every day.

- Express gratitude daily. Each night before bed you can make a written, verbal, or mental list of all the things that you are grateful for in your life. The more you express gratitude for the blessings in your life, the more of those blessings you will manifest.

- Talk to your baby every day. Research has shown that babies can hear our voices in the womb beginning at about five months. Play music for your baby, sing to him, or simply tell him how much you love him and how excited you are for his arrival. Your relationship with your baby begins in the womb. Respond to your baby's kicks and movement by rubbing your belly and saying "hello!"

- Set an intention that as you parent your baby you are also re-parenting yourself and receiving all the love, care, and consciousness that you give to your child.

- Set up your home and life so you can take the first forty days with your baby to sleep, heal, and be completely available to this incredible gift. Let your partner, friends, and family know that you will be taking this time with your baby and get in place whatever support systems you need, such as a professional, friend, or family member to help take care of you and your home.

Spending time in nature is a wonderful way to welcome your baby into the world.

Bibliography

Further Reading / Information

Caring for a Newborn/Parenting

Gordon, Jay. *Listening to Your Baby*. New York: Perigree, 2002.

Hogg, Tracy. *The Baby Whisperer*. New York: Ballantine Books, 2001.

Karp, Harvey. *The Happiest Baby on the Block*. New York: Bantam Dell, 2002.

Teich, Jessica and Barndel France de Bravo. *Trees Make the Best Mobiles*. New York: St. Martin's Griffin, 2002.

Weissbluth, Marc. *Healthy Sleep Habits, Happy Child*. New York: Ballantine, 1987.

Clutter Clearing and Organization

Allen, David. *Getting Things Done*. New York: Penguin Books, 2003.

Cilley, Marla. *Sink Reflections*. New York: Bantam Dell Books, 2002.

Kingston, Karen. *Clear Your Clutter with Feng Shui*. New York: Broadway Books, 1999.

Morgenstern, Julie. *Organizing from the Inside Out*. New York: Henry Holt and Company, 1998.

St. James, Elaine. *Simplify Your Life*. New York: Hyperion, 1994.

Feng Shui

Barrett, Jayme. *Feng Shui Your Life*. New York: Sterling Publishing Company, Inc., 2003.

Chin, R.D. *Feng Shui Revealed*. New York: Clarkson Potter, 1998.

Collins, Terah Kathryn. *The Western Guide to Feng Shui*. Carlsbad, CA: Hay House, Inc., 1996.

Collins, Terah Kathryn. *The Western Guide to Feng Shui Room by Room*. Carlsbad, CA: Hay House, Inc., 1999.

Lazenby, Gina. *Feng Shui House Book*. New York: Watson-Guptill, 1998.

Shurety, Sarah. *Feng Shui for Your Home*. United Kingdom: Rider, 1997.
Stasney, Sharon. *Feng Shui Chic*. New York: Sterling Publishing Company, Inc., 2000.

Healing Home
Alexander, Jane. *Spirit of the Home*. New York: Watson Guptill Publications, 2000.
Alexander, Jane. *Spirit of the Nursery*. New York: Watson Guptill Publications, 2002.
Crawford, Ilse. *The Sensual Home*. New York: Rizzoli International Publications, 1998.
Lazenby, Gina. *The Healing Home*. Guilford, CT: The Lyons Press, 2001.
Moran, Victoria. *Shelter for the Spirit*. New York: Perennial, 1998.
Pegrum, Juliet. *Peace at Home*. San Francisco: Chronicle Books, 2003.

Healthy Home
Berthold-Bond, Annie. *Clean and Green*. Woodstock, NY: Ceres Press, 1990.
Dadd, Debra Lynn. *Home Safe Home*. New York: Tarcher/Penguin, 1997.
Ikramuddin, Aisha and Mindy Pennybaker. *Mothers and Others for a Livable Planet: Guide to Natural Baby Care*. New York: John Wiley and Sons, 1999.
Laporte, Paula Baker, Erica Elliot, and John Banta. *Prescriptions for a Healthy House*. British Columbia, Canada: New Society Publishers, 2001.
Nassif, Monica. *Spring Cleaning: The Spirit of Keeping Home*. San Francisco: Chronicle Books, 2003.
Pearson, David. *The New Natural House Book*. New York: Fireside/Simon and Schuster, 1998.
Phillips, Dan. *Designs for a Healthy Home*. San Francisco: Soma Books, 2002.
Pottkotter, Louis, M.D. *The Natural Nursery*. Chicago: Contemporary Books, 1994.
Seo, Danny. *Conscious Style Home*. New York: St. Martin's Press, 2001.
Thompson, Athena. *Homes that Heal*. Canada: New Society Publications, 2004.

Interior Design
Bellissimo, Wendy. *Nesting*. Chicago: NVU Editions, LLC, 2003.
Strand, Jessica. *Baby's Room*. San Francisco: Chronicle Books, 2002.

Plants
Wolverton, Dr. B. C. *How to Grow Fresh Air: 50 House Plants that Purify Your Home or Office*. New York: Penguin Books, 1996.

Pregnancy
Eisenberg, Arlene, Heidi E. Murkoff, and Sandee E. Hathaway. *What to Expect When You Are Expecting*. New York: Simon and Schuster, 1984.
Khalsa, Gurmukh Kaur. *Bountiful, Beautiful, Blissful: Experience the Natural Power of Pregnancy and Birth with Kundalini Yoga and Meditation*. New York: St. Martin's Press, 2003.

Self-Help/Inspiration

Baker, Dan. *What Happy People Know*. New York: St. Martin's Griffin, 2003.

Jeffers, Susan. *Feel the Fear and Do It Anyway*. New York: Rizzoli International, Ballantine Books, 1988.

Space Clearing

Kingston, Karen. *Creating Sacred Space with Feng Shui*. New York: Bantam Doubleday Dell, 1997.

Linn, Denise. *Sacred Space*. New York: McGraw Hill/Contemporary, 2001.

Linn, Denise. *Space Clearing A–Z: How to Use Feng Shui to Purify and Bless Your Home*. Carlsbad, CA: Hay House, Inc., 2001.

Informational Websites and Periodicals

For more information about Life Design consultations:
The Art of Everyday Living: www.artofeverydayliving.com

For locating a Feng Shui consultant in your area or for training:
Western School of Feng Shui: www.wsfs.com

For locating a space clearing practitioner in your area or for training:
Denise Linn: www.deniselinn.com
Karen Kingston: www.spaceclearing.com

For contacting a professional organizer:
National Association of Professional Organizers: www.napo.net

For information on creating a healthy home:
Children's Health Environmental Coalition: www.checnet.org
Environmental Protection Agency: www.epa.gov
The Green Guide: www.thegreenguide.com
Greenpeace: www.greenpeaceusa.org
Natural Home Magazine: Loveland, CO. Natural Home LLC
Organic Style Magazine: Emmaus, PA. Rodale, Inc., 2004.

For contacting a healthy home consultant:
H3 Environmental Corporation: www.H3Environmental.com, 818.766.1787
12439 Magnolia Blvd., Box 263, Valley Village, CA 91607

For information on clutter clearing:
The Fly Lady, Martha Cilley: www.flylady.com

For information about Spiritual Psychology:
University of Santa Monica: www.gousm.edu

For contacting an EMF consultant:
EMF Services: www.emfservices.com
International Institute for Bau-Biologie and Ecology Inc.: 727.461.4371,
www.bau-biologieusa.com

For baby safety tips:
American Academy of Pediatrics: www.aap.org
Juvenile Products Manufacturers Association: www.jpma.org
National Highway Traffic Safety Administration (NHTSA): www.nhtsa.dot.gov
   (for car seat information)
National Safety Council website: www.nsc.org

Resources

Products

All Around Baby Stores:
Babies-R-Us: www.babiesrus.com
Baby Center: www.babycenter.com
Babystyle: 877.378.9537, www.babystyle.com

Bath De-Chlorinator:
Harmony: 800.869.3446, www.gaiam.com
Lifekind: 800.284.4983, www.lifekind.com

Diapers:
Tushies Diapers (gel, laytex, dye and perfume free disposable diapers): 800.344.6379,
www.tushies.com or Whole Foods www.wholefoods.com for store locations

Dust Mite Covers:
Allergy Control Products: 800.422.3878
Organic Dust Mite Barrier Covers: 800.596.7450, www.ecobaby.com

EMF Products:
Less EMF.com: www.lessemf.com

Feng Shui Crystals and Other Traditional Enhancements:
From Wind to Water: 813.961.5600, www.fromwindtowater.com
Western School of Feng Shui Store: www.efsgallery.com

Furniture, Curtains, Rugs, Storage, and More:
Ikea: 800.434.IKEA (4532), www.ikea.com
Land of Nod: 800.933.9904, www.landofnod.com
Pottery Barn Kids: 800.430.7373, www.potterybarnkids.com

Glass Bottles:
Baby Center: www.babycenter.com
The Natural Baby Catalog: 888.550.2460, www.kidsstuff.com

Moses Basket with Organic and Cotton Wool Lining:
Little Merry Fellows: 203.270.1820, www.littlemerryfellows.com

Natural Cleaning Products:
Caldrea All Natural Cleaning Products: www.caldrea.com
Green Home: www.greenhome.com
Harmony: 800.869.3446, www.gaiam.com
Trader Joe's: www.traderjoes.com, or other organic and natural food markets
Whole Foods: www.wholefoods.com (for store locations)

Natural Paints, Sealers, and Other Non-Toxic Building Products:
Environmental Home Center: 800.281.9785, www.environmentalhomecenter.com
Green Home: www.greenhome.com
Living Green: 310.838.8442, www.livingreen.com, 8675 Washington Blvd., Culver City, CA 90232
AFM: 800.239.0321, www.AFMsafecoat.com

Organic Baby Skincare:
Babybecause: 866.734.2634, www.babybecause.com
Lifekind: 800.284.4983, www.lifekind.com
The Natural Baby Catalog: 888.550.2460, www.kidsstuff.com
Whole Foods: www.wholefoods.com (for store locations)

Organic Baby Stores (Baby Clothes, Crib Linens, Cribs, Wool Mattresses, Wool Puddle Pads, and Furnishings):
Babybecause: 866.734.2634, www.babybecause.com
Coyuchi: 888.418.8847, www.coyuchi.com
Green Home: www.greenhome.com
Lifekind: 800.284.4983, www.lifekind.com
The Natural Baby Catalog: 888.550.2460, www.kidsstuff.com
Under the Nile: 800.883.4402, www.underthenile.com

Organic Bumper Fill and Bumper Cover:
Pure Beginnings: 866.Pur-Baby, www.purebeginnings.com

Organic Cotton Cloth Diapers and Wipes:
BabyBecause: 866.734.2634, www.babybecause.com
The Natural Baby Catalog: 888.550.2460, www.kidsstuff.com

Organic Cotton Play Mats:
Harmony: 800.869.3446, www.gaiam.com
Lifekind: 800.284.4983, www.lifekind.com
The Natural Baby Catalog: 888.550.2460, www.kidsstuff.com
Sage Creek Naturals: 866.598.1400, www.sagecreeknaturals.com

Organic Wool Mattresses with No Metal:
H3 Environmental Corporation: 818.766.1787, www.H3Environmental.com, 12439
Magnolia Blvd., Box 263, Valley Village, CA 91607

Organization:
The Container Store: 888.266.8246, www.thecontainerstore.com
Hold Everything: 888.922.4117, www.holdeverything.com
Organized Living (store locations only): www.organizedliving.com
Remember That: www.rememberthatmoment.com (custom home video editing)

Space Clearing Tools:
For bells: www.spaceclearing.com
For sage sticks: Whole Foods: www.wholefoods.com (for store locations) or other
natural grocery/ health food stores
For essential oils: Whole Foods: www.wholefoods.com (for store locations) or Small
Flower: www.smallflower.com

Wind Chimes:
WindChime.com: 800.727.3350, www.windchime.com

Wood Baby Clothes Hangers:
The Natural Baby Catalog: 888.550.2460, www.kidsstuff.com

Wood Toys:
Back to Basics Catalog: 800.356.5360, www.backtobasicstoys.com
Magic Cabin: 888.623.6557 for catalog
The Michael Olaf Company: Call for the Joyful Child Catalog, 888.880.9235

Wool Crib Mattresses and Custom Wool and Cotton Cradle/Bassinet/Co-sleeper
    Mattresses:
Crown City Mattress: 626.796.9101
Lifekind: 800.284.4983, www.lifekind.com

All Photography by Tamara Muth-King.

All prints originally developed by SMC Labs, Santa Monica, California.

Cover: Crib from Room with a View, 310.998.5858; organic crib linens by Coyuchi, www.coyuchi.com; 100% organic cotton fill and cover bumper by Sage Creek Naturals, www.sagecreeknaturals.com; crib blanket from Baby Because, www.babybecause.com. Fabric for curtains from Diamond Fabric, 323.931.8148; Custom-made Painted Wood giraffe by Mohaupt Woodworks, 520.886.9806.

ii) Crib and changing pad by Bellini's 888.772.2291, www.bellini.com; crib linens custom made; antique dresser, basket, Cost Plus World Market, www.costplus.com; floor cushions, ABC Carpet and Home, www.abchome.com; mobile from the Acorn Store, 310.451.5845.

xiv) Wood toy from the Acorn Store, 310.451.5845.

2) Crib from Room with a View, 310.998.5858; organic crib linens by Coyuchi, www.coyuchi.com; 100 percent organic cotton fill bumper by Sage Creek Naturals, www.sagecreeknaturals.com; crib blanket from Baby Because, www.babybecause.com; hand-me-down teddy bear.

4) See page 85 listing.

6) Wicker bassinet from Room with a View, 310.998.5858; handmade quilt from Room with a View, 310.998.5858; organic wool fill and cotton cover bassinet mattress (not shown) by Crown City Mattress, 626.796.9101.

20) Crib from Pottery Barn Kids, www.potterybarnkids.com; crib linens and bumper by Amy Coe, www.amycoe.com; nursing chair fabric by Lulu DK, 212.223.4234, www.luludk.com.

30) Changing table and caddy by Thea Segal, 310.207.2577; hamper from Waterworks, 310.246.9766; mobile from the Acorn Store, 310.451.5845; ABC/123 art, handmade.

33) Storage bins from the Container Store, www.containerstore.com.

40) Rug, bookshelf, red bins, and orange lamp all from Ikea, www.ikea.com; pillow fabric is homemade.

49) Sage stick from Whole Foods; similar Space Clearing bells may be purchased from www.spaceclearing.com.

52) See page 80 listing.

56) Crib from Ikea, www.ikea.com; painted animal blocks, Babystyle, www.babystyle.com; antique dresser; wheatgrass can be found at Whole Foods.

58) Crib from Room with a View, 310.998.5858; crib fabric, nursing chair fabric, and pillow fabric from Imagine That, 310.395.9553; sofa from Sofa U Love; toy chest is a family piece.

63) Tablecloth from Ikea, www.ikea.com; kitchen chair by Eames, www.office designs.com; wood toys from Back to Basics, 800.356.5360.

66) Multi-faceted round crystal, Essential Feng Shui® Gallery, www.efsgallery.com.

68) See page 2 listing.

71) Fabric for curtains and chair from Diamond Fabric, 323.931.8148; chair from Fun Furniture, 323.655.2711; hand-me-down teddy bear.

74) Changing table, shelf, caddy, and lamp from Auntie Barbara's Antiques, 310.285.0873. Interior design by Jenna Grosfeld, Los Angeles, CA, 310.441.3060.

76) Duck stool and rug from Pottery Barn Kids, potterybarnkids.com.

80) Crib from Fun Furniture, 323.655.2711; rug from Pottery Barn Kids, potterybarnkids.com; crib linens, "Traditions" by Pamela Kline from Imagine That, 310.395.9553; curtain fabric by Calvin to the trade only; ottoman by Dutalier from Fun Furniture, 323.655.2711; and ottoman fabric "Staten Ticking Stripe Red" by Jane Shelton to the trade. Interior design by Nancy Langdon, 323.654.8901.

85) Wood hangers from The Natural Baby Catalog, 888.550.2460.

90) Diapers from Tushies, 800.344.6379; woven basket and liner from Land of Nod, 800.933.9904; quilt from Room with a View, 310.998.5858.

93) Bookcase by Thea Segal, 310.207.2577; organic cotton fill futon mat and cover from Harmony, 800.869.3446; pull duck toy from www.geniusbabies.com; rainbow rings from the Acorn Store, 310.451.5845; pull frog available at babyscholars.com; painted wood blocks from Babystyle, www.babystyle.com; organic white bear from Lifekind, 800.284.4983, www.lifekind.com; red car with people from the Acorn Store, 310.451.5845.

99) Hot air balloon from Ballard Designs, www.ballarddesigns.com; corner shelf originally designed by Mohaupt Woodworks, 520.886.9806; hand-me-down teddy bear.

102) Crib by Pottery Barn Kids, potterybarnkids.com; crib linens by Amy Coe, www.amycoe.com.

116) Antique dresser, antique chair, and chair fabric by Michael Levine, www.mlfabrics.com; curtain fabric hand-embroidered from India; cushions, ABC Carpet and Home, www.abchome.com; bear, FAO Schwarz, 800.426.8697; antique Persian rug.

118) Bookcase from Plummers, www.plummersfurniture.com; baskets and rod with clips from Ikea, www.ikea.com.

120) See page 74 listing.

123) Wood cradle from the Juvenile Shop, 818.986.6214. Interior design by Jenna Grosfeld, 310.441.3060.

127) Red toy basket found by owner.

131) Angel Sleeping sign, www.babyultimate.com.

136) See page 93 listing.

139) Green tray from Pottery Barn, www.potterybarnkids.com; handmade rocks; beeswax candle from Whole Foods, www.wholefoods.com for store locations.

153) Moses basket from Babystyle, www.babystyle.com; vintage blanket found at flea market.

Index

A

Action steps, taking, 15
Adoptions, 144
Adult bedrooms, 38–39, 122, 130, 132–34
Affirmations, 12, 18, 88, 91, 92, 96, 119
"Affirmative prayer," 15
Air quality, 11, 55, 66
    and air filters, 55
Allen, David, 25
Allergies, 134, 135
Art of Everyday Living, 2
Artwork
    and Bagua, 112, 115, 117
    and balanced energy flow, 64–65
    in changing area, 74
    and enhancing the nursery, 92, 94–95, 96, 97, 100–101, 102, 104
    and safety, 54
    and sleep, 125, 126, 135
Asking for help, 147–48, 152

B

Baby
    building relationship with, 143–44, 152

communication with, 107, 143–44, 152
    organizing and preparing for the, 70–71
    what you will need for the, 69–88
Baby bags, 87
Baby monitors, 79
Baby-proofing homes, 53–54, 62–64, 67
BabyBjorn, 84
Backpacks, 87
Bagua, 105–19
Bagua Map
    applying the, 109–12, 119
    areas of, 106–9
    enhancements, 115–18
    "missing" areas in, 112–13, 115
    in nursery, 114–18
    overview of, 105–6
    and quick tips, 119
    and your life, 113–14
Baker, Dan, 138
Balance
    and Bagua, 109, 115
    and enhancing the nursery, 100–101, 103
Bassinets, 6, 77, 78, 79, 130

Bathing area, items you will need for, 75–76
Bathrooms, 65, 96, 98, 113, 114, 133
Baths/bathtubs, 75–76, 122
Bau-biologie, 9, 61
Beams/slanted ceilings, 65–66
Bedrooms
   adult, 38–39, 65, 77, 122, 130, 132–34, 135
   healthy, 134, 135
Beds
  in adult bedroom, 133
  and changing needs, 150
  in nursery, 85–86
  See also Cribs
Bedtime, routines at, 86, 122–23, 125, 129, 135
Being in the moment, 144–45, 148
Being the most of who you are, 141–42
Bells, and preparing the nursery, 48
Berthold-Bond, Annie, 46
Big rooms, 101–2
Birth announcements, 85
Black, 43, 117, 118
Blankets, 78, 81, 84, 86, 87, 88, 135
Blessings, 22, 107, 115, 116–18, 139, 152
  and the nursery, 50–51
Blue, 42, 100–101, 116, 117
Bottle sterilizer, 72
Bottle warmer, 71, 72
Bottles, 71, 72, 87
Bouncy seats, 81
Breast pump, 71, 72
Bumpers, 78, 123, 128
Burp clothes, 71, 72, 73–74

C
Car seats, 70, 84, 87, 88
  and Child Passenger Safety Technician, 70

Carbon monoxide detector, 39, 51, 53
Career
  and Bagua, 105, 109, 112, 113, 114, 118
  and example of Life Design, 14
Ceiling fans, 54, 125–26
Ceilings, slanted, 65–66
Challenges, and preparing your home, 29–30
Change, and preparing yourself, 150–52
Changing area, 73–75
Changing pad, 84, 87
Changing table, 30, 71, 73, 74, 75, 86, 95, 125
Chemicals
  in adult bedrooms, 134
  and health and safety, 55, 57, 66
  in home, 11
  and items you will need, 72
  in play area, 79, 81
  and preparing the nursery, 46
  and sleep, 77, 135
  See also Toxins; PVCs; VOCs
Children
  and Bagua, 105, 107, 108, 115, 117
  and teaching children about clutter, 34–35
Children's Health Environmental Coalition, 45, 73
Cilley, Marla, 30
"Clap" the nursery, 48
Cleaning
  and Bagua, 114
  of bottles, 72
  of clutter, 19–21, 26–30, 150
  and health and safety, 46, 51, 55, 57
  and preparing the nursery, 37, 46, 51
  and preparing yourself, 138
  products for, 46, 51, 55
Cleansing, energy, 46–50, 51, 129
Clocks, 71, 72, 117

Clothes
  and changing needs, 150
  as gifts, 82
  and items you will need, 69, 71,
    82–83, 88
  and packing for hospital, 84
  storage of, 82, 84–85, 88, 150
  and travel, 86, 87
Clutter
  and Bagua, 113–14
  and balanced energy flow, 66, 67
  challenges concerned with, 29–30
  changing habits that create, 33–34
  and changing needs, 150
  clearing out, 19–21, 26–30, 150
  effect of, 7
  and Feng Shui, 10
  "free spirit," 29–30
  and items you will need, 69
  meditation as clearing, 26–28
  not-accepting-myself-now, 24
  and packing for hospital, 84
  reasons for accumulating, 23–24
  and sleep, 128
  teaching children about, 34–35
  twelve steps concerned with, 26–28,
    30
  types of, 23–26
Collins, Terah Kathryn, 22
Color
  and Bagua, 115–18
  balance of, 100–101
  and balanced energy flow, 66
  and enhancing the nursery, 95, 99,
    100–102
  and harmonious homes, 103
  and preparing the nursery, 41–43, 51
  and size of nursery, 101–2
  and sleep, 126
Comfort
  importance of, 53

  and safety, 53–67
Comfort zone, 61–64
Command Position, 38–39, 59, 60, 61,
    66, 67, 126, 133, 135
Convertible sofa beds, 85–86
Cordaro, Mary, 134
Cradle cap, 76
Cradles, 77, 79, 122
Creative enhancements, 98
Creativity
  and Bagua, 105, 108, 115, 117
  and enhancing the nursery, 92, 97, 98
Cribs
  and changing needs, 150
  and enhancing the nursery, 104
  and health and safety, 55, 57–58, 60,
    61, 66, 77–78
  location of, 60, 61, 66, 126, 128,
    135
  objects over, 125
  as play areas, 125
  portable, 78
  transition to, 123
  and travel, 86
  used, 57–58
  views from, 96, 104, 126, 135
Crystals, 65, 66, 96, 98–99, 112, 113
Curtains, 55, 99, 115, 125, 128

D

Danger
  actual, 53–54, 66
  perceived, 53, 54–55, 65, 66
Decorating
  from the heart, 89–91
  as opportunity to enhance your life,
    105
Designing your life. *See* Bagua Map
Diaper pails, 74, 75, 86
Diapers, 71, 73, 75, 86, 87, 91
Doulas, 130

Dreams
    Bagua Map as vessel for manifesting,
        106
    and clearing out clutter, 21
    getting in touch with, 12
    and living with what you love, 22
    and preparing your home, 36
    and preparing yourself, 139

E

Eaves, 65–66
Electronic equipment, 132–33, 135
EMFs (electric and magnetic fields),
    60–61, 71, 86, 129, 132–33
Energy
    and adult bedrooms, 132
    balanced flow of, 64–67
    as basic Feng Shui principle, 10
    and changing needs, 150
    and clearing out clutter, 19, 21, 30
    and enhancing the nursery, 91–92, 94,
        96–99
    flow of, 66, 112, 128
    and living with what you love, 21
    and packing for hospital, 83
    and preparing the nursery, 40, 42, 50,
        51
    and preparing yourself, 139, 140, 141,
        148
    and safety and health, 55, 64–67
    and sleep, 122, 128
    See also Bagua Map
Energy cleansing, 46–50, 51, 129
Enhancements
    and Bagua, 112, 114, 115–18
    creative, 98
    and sleep, 126, 128
Environmental Protection Agency, 44,
    55, 57
Essential oils, 47–48
ExerSaucers, 81

Expectations, 130, 135, 148–50
Expensive items, letting go of, 25–26

F

Fame and reputation, 105, 107, 112,
    117
Family
    and asking for help, 147, 152
    and Bagua, 105, 106–7, 108, 115,
        116
    and example of Life Design, 13
    See also Photographs
Fear-based clutter, 23–24
Feelings
    and enhancing the nursery, 89–90
    making list of, 89–90, 104, 142
Feng Shui, 1–2, 9–10, 38, 54, 64–65,
    91, 96, 98, 99–100, 133
    See also Bagua Map
Finances
    and example of Life Design, 14
    See also Wealth and prosperity
First aid kit, 84
Floors
    and Bagua, 115
    and balanced energy flow, 65
    and enhancing the nursery, 99, 101
    and harmonious homes, 103
    and health, 55
    in play area, 81, 82
    and preparing the nursery, 44–45, 51
    and size of nursery, 101
Flowers, 48, 50, 95
    See also Plants
Focusing, 12, 15–16
Forgiveness, 107, 142
"the forty days," 146–47, 152
Fountains, 98, 118
"Free spirit" clutter, 29–30
Friends, 13, 108, 147, 152
    See also Helpful People

Front doors, 109, 112
Furniture
    arrangement/location of, 10, 59–61,
        65, 66, 67, 112
    and Bagua, 115, 116
    and balance, 101
    and balanced energy flow, 65, 66, 67
    comfortable, 58–59
    and comfortable homes, 62–63
    and enhancing the nursery, 95, 99,
        101
    excess, 66
    and Feng Shui, 10
    and health and safety, 54–55, 56,
        57–58, 59
    and items you will need, 71
    in play area, 81
    and preparing the nursery, 39
    and preparing yourself, 138
    sharp angles/edges on, 54–55, 59,
        128
    and size of nursery, 101
    and sleep, 125, 128
    slipcovers for, 62–63, 67
    storage of, 32
    used, 57–58, 116

G

Gifts
    and Bagua, 107, 116
    clothes as, 82
    and enhancing the nursery, 94
    and preparing the nursery, 50
    registering for, 34, 84, 88, 138
    unwanted, 25
Goals
    and creating a Life Design, 15
    defining, 12
    and enhancing the nursery, 91, 92
    focusing on realizing, 15
    and living with what you love, 22, 23

    and preparing your home, 36
    and preparing yourself, 139
    reviewing, 15
    writing down, 12
    See also Intentions
Gordon, Jay, 131–32
Gratitude, 138–40, 152
Gray, 117
Green, 42, 65, 116, 117
The Green Guide, 72
Greenpeace, 81
Grooming kit, 75
Gurmukh, Sikh, 146

H

Habits, that create clutter, 33–34
Hallways, 65
Harmony, 100, 103
Health
    and Bagua, 105, 106–7, 109, 116,
        118
    and example of Life Design, 13
    and furniture, 57–58
    and healthy homes, 10–11
    and healthy nursery, 55–57
    and preparing the nursery, 50
    and preparing yourself, 143
    See also Safety; VOCs; EMFs
Help
    asking for, 147–48, 152
    receiving, 130–32
Helpful People, 105, 108, 112, 115,
    117
HEPA/carbon filters, 55–56
    and HEPA vacuum/air filters, 45, 55
High chairs, 86
Home
    baby-proofing, 53–54, 62–64, 67
    comfortable, 61–64
    connection between well-being and, 2,
        3, 7, 9

Home (*cont'd*)
  and designing your life, 8–9
  and example of Life Design, 13
  as extension of body, 10–11
  as feeling, 5, 17
  harmonious, 103
  healthy, 10–11
  maker of, 151
  as opportunity for change, 8
  as physical place, 5
  preparing your, 19–36
  and preparing yourself, 138
  and quality of life, 2, 3
  as reflection of you, 7, 9, 22
  as supportive environment, 3, 5, 8, 31
  as telling story of your life, 18
  tour of, 144
  welcoming your baby, 1–3
  you and your, 7–8
Homemaker, 151
Hospital, packing for, 83–84
Humor, sense of, 147–48

I

Immune system, 134
Inheritances, unwanted items from, 25
Inspiration boards, 90, 104
Institute for Bau-Biologie and Ecology, 61
Intentions
  and Bagua, 106, 112, 115, 116, 119
  clarifying, 12
  and clearing out clutter, 21, 26, 28
  discovering, 11–12
  and enhancing the nursery, 96, 100
  and preparing the nursery, 48
  and preparing yourself, 141, 142, 152
  resetting, 28
  reviewing, 15
  and sleep, 124, 129

  and storage, 32
  and travel, 88
  vocalizing, 124
  writing down, 12
  See also Goals
Intuition/instincts, 7, 18, 38, 141
Items you will need, 69–89

J

"Just in case" scenarios, 23–24
Juvenile Products Manufacturers
  Association, 77

K

Karp, Harvey, 123
Kingston, Karen, 23
Kitchen, nursing items for, 72
Knowledge, and Bagua, 105, 108–9, 112, 115, 117

L

Lamps. *See* Light/lamps
Lap pad, 73, 75
Laundry hampers, 75
Lavender, 43
Lead paint, 44, 51, 55, 58
Letters, as challenge for clearing out clutter, 29
Letting go, 15, 16, 21, 23, 25–26, 35, 137–38, 140, 142, 145
Life
  decorating as opportunity to enhance, 105
  designing your, 8–9
Life coaching techniques, 2
Life Design
  creating a, 12–17, 18
  example of, 13–15
  overview about, 2–4
  reviewing, 18
Lifestyle, 13, 61–62

Light/lamps
  and Bagua, 112, 117, 118
  and balanced energy flow, 65, 66
  and enhancing the nursery, 95, 97, 101
  and items you will need, 71, 72
  and preparing the nursery, 45
  and size of nursery, 101
  and sleep, 128–29
Linn, Denise, 49
Love
  and Bagua, 105, 107–8, 112–13, 114, 116, 117
  and enhancing the nursery, 89, 92, 96, 103
  importance of, 17
  living with what you, 21–23
  meaningful objects and things you, 92, 94
  nursery as expression of, 17
  and packing for hospital, 83
  and preparing the nursery, 37, 42, 50
  and preparing your home, 36
  and preparing yourself, 137, 138, 140, 142, 143, 144, 145, 152
  self-love, 22, 107
  unconditional, 108, 117

M

Material blessings, 22
Mattresses, 55, 77, 78, 79, 134, 150
Meditation, 15–16, 26–28, 42
"Mental clutter," 15, 24–25, 36
"Mind sweep," 25
Mirrors, 64, 79, 82, 97–98, 102, 112, 113, 126, 128
Mistakes
  as challenge for clearing out clutter, 29
  forgiving, 142
  making, 29
  and preparing yourself, 142

Mobiles
  and Bagua, 117, 118
  in changing area, 74, 75
  and enhancing the nursery, 98
  in play area, 82
  and safety, 54
  and sleep, 122, 125, 135
Moses basket, 78, 79
Murals. *See* Artwork
Music, 82, 83, 88, 98, 152

N

Naps, 78, 122–23, 125
National Highway Traffic Safety Administration, 70
National Lead Information Center, 44
National Safety Council, 58, 77
Nature
  and enhancing the nursery, 95, 99–100, 104
  five elements in, 99–100
  imitating, 99
Night nurses, 130
Nursery
  activities in, 125
  Bagua Map in, 114–18
  beds in, 85–86
  blessing the, 50–51
  changing needs in, 150–51
  cleaning the, 37, 46, 51, 138
  color for, 41–43, 51, 100–101
  and decorating from the heart, 89–91
  energy cleansing of, 46–50, 51, 129
  enhancing the, 89–104, 115–18
  as expression of love, 17
  as harmonious, 103
  healthy, 55–57
  location of, 37–40, 51, 129
  painting of, 37, 43–44, 55, 56, 138
  preparing the, 3, 37–52
  renovating and repairing the, 40–41

Nursery (*cont'd*)
    setting up of, 70, 138
    size of, 101–2
    womb-like atmosphere in, 3, 5, 7, 123
    See also Sleep
Nursing area, items you will need in,
    71–72
Nursing bras, 72
Nursing chair, 59, 60, 61, 71, 72, 99

O

Objects
    and Bagua, 112, 114, 115–18
    and enhancing the nursery, 92, 94, 104
    meaningful, 92, 94, 104, 114, 115–18
    over cribs, 125
    and packing for hospital, 83
    pairs of, 117
    and sleep, 122, 125
One year rule, 28
Orange, 43, 101
Organization
    and clearing out clutter, 27, 28
    and items you will need, 70–71
    of photographs, 85
    and preparing your home, 19, 27, 28,
    31, 36
Outings, 84

P

Paint/painting
    and balanced energy flow, 66
    of beams and eaves, 66
    and enhancing the nursery, 101–2
    and health, 44, 51, 55, 56, 58
    lead, 44, 51, 55, 58
    of nursery, 37, 43–44, 55, 56, 138
    and preparing yourself, 138
    and size of nursery, 101–2
Parenting
    books about, 135, 148
    classes about, 147
    as meaningful job, 145
    by own parents, 142
    and preparing yourself, 144
    re-parenting, 142, 152
    style of, 70
Parents
    and example of Life Design, 14
    as models, 107, 109, 141, 149–50
    perfect, 141–42
    role of, 151
Partners
    and adult bedrooms, 132
    and bed in nursery, 86
    expectations of, 130, 135, 148–50
    help from, 130
    and packing for hospital, 83
    and preparing yourself, 148–50
    relationship with, 148–50
Patterns, and enhancing the nursery, 95,
    102–3
Phone numbers, 84
Photographs
    and adult bedrooms, 133
    and Bagua, 115, 116, 117
    as challenge for clearing out clutter, 29
    and enhancing the nursery, 92, 94, 97,
    104
    organization of, 85
    and packing for hospital, 83
Pink, 42, 100–101, 117
Plants, 65, 95, 97, 98, 104, 112, 113,
    116, 117
    See also Flowers
Plastic, 72, 73, 77, 79, 81, 87
Play
    area for, 63, 74, 79–82
    and changing area, 74
    items you will need for, 79–82
    and sleep, 122, 124–28, 135
Power Position. *See* Command Position

Prayer, 15–16
  See also Meditation
Pregnancy and birth experience, and
  example of Life Design, 14
Preparing yourself
  and asking for help, 147–48
  and being in the moment, 144–45
  and being the most of who you are,
    141–42
  and building a relationship with your
    baby, 143–44
  and change, 150–51
  and deciding you're ready, 137–38
  and the forty days, 146–47
  and gratitude, 138–40
  and quick tips, 152
  and role of parent and maker of home,
    151
  and self-nurturing, 140–41
  and your partner, 148–50
Priorities, reevaluating, 145
Puddle pads, 77, 78, 79
Purple, 43, 117
PVCs (polyvinyl chlorides), 79, 81

Q

Quick tips
  and Bagua, 119
  and being at home, 18
  and comfort and safety, 67
  and designing your life, 119
  and enhancing the nursery, 104
  and preparing the nursery, 51
  and preparing your home, 36
  and preparing yourself, 152
  and sleep, 135
  and what you will need, 88

R

Readiness, 137–38
Red, 40, 42, 117

Reframing, 131–32
Registration, for gifts, 34, 84, 88, 138
Relationships
  and Bagua, 105, 107–8, 112–13, 114,
    117
  and building a relationship with your
    baby, 143–44, 152
  and enhancing the nursery, 92, 94
  and example of Life Design, 13
  with partners, 148–50
Religion, 138
Renovations and repairs, 40–41
Reputation, and Bagua, 105, 107, 112,
    117
Romance, 133, 135
Rooms
  size of, 101–2
  use of, 61–62, 66
Routines, bedtime, 86, 122–23, 125,
    129, 135
Rugs. *See* Floors

S

Safety
  and balanced energy flow, 65–66
  and car seats, 70, 84, 87, 88
  and comfort, 53–67
  of cribs, 77–78
  See also EMFs; VOCs
Self-actualization, 109
Self-cultivation, and Bagua, 105, 108–9,
    112, 115, 117
Self-esteem, 59, 91, 92
Self-improvement, 109
Self-love, 22
Self-nurturing, 22, 132, 140–41, 142,
    146, 148, 152
Senses, stimulation of, 95
Shampoos and body washes, 76
Sharp angles/edges, 54–55, 59, 63–64,
    77, 101, 128

Sheets, 77–78, 79, 88, 123, 128, 129, 134, 135
Shoes, 66
Siblings, 94, 104
  and sharing a room, 37–38
Side tables, 71–72, 133
Sikh religion, 146
Simplifying
  and preparing your home, 19, 36
  See also Clutter
Sleep
  and bedtime routines, 86, 122–23, 125, 129, 135
  deprivation of, 121–22, 130, 131, 132, 135
  and energy cleansing, 129
  and enhancing the nursery, 97
  importance of, 121
  and play, 122, 124–28, 135
  and quick tips, 135
  and receiving help, 130–32
  and self-nurturing, 146
  and sleeping rooms, 124–28
  and travel, 86, 87, 88
  See also Naps
Sleeping area, items you will need for, 77–79
Slings, 87
Small rooms, 101–2
Smell, 95
Smoke, 47–48
Smoke detectors, 53
Sound, in sleeping room, 129
Staircases, 64–65
Storage
  and Bagua, 113, 114
  and changing needs, 150
  for clothes, 82, 84–85, 88, 150
  and clutter, 31–33, 36
  and items you will need, 72, 88
  in play area, 81, 82

  and sleep, 125, 126, 135
  for toys, 125, 126, 127, 135, 150
Stress, 97, 138, 140
Strollers, 84, 87
Support, 108, 115, 143, 147–48, 152
Swaddling babies, 130
Swings, 81

T
Teething, 87
Televisions, 126, 132, 133, 135
Themes, and enhancing the nursery, 102–3
Toilets, 96, 98, 113
"Tone" the nursery, 48
Touch, 95
Towels and washclothes, 76
Toxins, 10–11, 43–44, 51, 55–56, 57, 72, 77–78, 79, 81
  See also Chemicals, PVCs; VOCs
Toys
  in adult bedrooms, 132
  in bathing area, 75, 76
  in changing area, 74
  and changing needs, 150
  and clutter, 34, 35
  color of, 126
  and comfortable homes, 62
  and energy cleansing, 129
  and enhancing the nursery, 93, 98, 99
  plastic, 79, 81
  in play area, 79, 81, 82
  and sleep, 78, 122, 124, 125, 126, 127, 129, 135
  storage for, 125, 126, 127, 135, 150
  and travel, 86
Travel, 86–88

U

Unconditional love, 108, 117

V

Vacuums, 45
Vastu, 9
Ventilation, 55–56, 66
Views
    in adult bedroom, 133
    in changing area, 74
    from cribs, 96, 104, 126, 135
    and enhancing the nursery, 96, 97,
     102, 104
    and location of furniture, 61
    "of the world," 79, 123
    and sleep, 122, 126, 135
    from windows, 96, 97, 102
Visual reminders, creating, 15, 16
Visualization, 12, 15, 16, 24
VOCs (Volatile organic compounds),
    43, 44, 51, 55–57

W

Water, images of, 98, 117, 118
Wealth and prosperity, and Bagua, 105,
    107, 113, 114, 116, 117
Weissbluth, Marc, 121
White, 40, 43, 100, 101, 117
White noise machines, 129
Wind chimes, 65, 95, 97–98, 117
Windows
    and Bagua, 112
    and balanced energy flow, 65
    and energy cleansing, 129
    and enhancing the nursery, 95, 96, 97,
     98, 102
    opening of, 55–56, 66, 95, 129, 137
    and sleep, 129
    views from, 96, 97, 102
Wipes, 71, 73, 75, 87

Y

Yellow, 42–43, 101, 118

Alison Forbes and Laura Forbes Carlin are sisters and co-owners of *The Art of Everyday Living*, a home and lifestyle consulting company. They specialize in Life Design, a unique service that combines Feng Shui, life coaching, interior decorating, and healthy living. They teach their clients how to design their ideal life by designing their ideal home.

Laura and Alison have studied Feng Shui, life coaching, and spiritual practices from teachers around the country. Laura holds a Master's degree in Spiritual Psychology from the University of Santa Monica and Alison has a Master's degree in Education from Harvard University. They are also both graduates of the Western School of Feng Shui™, and they live in Los Angeles, CA. Laura lives with her husband and son.

For more information on consultations and speaking engagements or to sign up for their newsletter, please visit www.artofeverydayliving.com.